ks due in two weeks from last

WITHDRAWN

ENGLAND IS A VILLAGE

The village under snow

ENGLAND IS A VILLAGE

By
C. HENRY WARREN

Illustrated by
DENYS
WATKINS PITCHFORD

New York
E. P. DUTTON & CO., INC.
1941

COPYRIGHT, 1941
BY E. P. DUTTON & CO., INC.
ALL RIGHTS RESERVED
PRINTED IN THE U. S. A.

First Edition

For Heinz

FOREWORD

THIS chronicle of village life was mainly written during the two months of comparative calm which were destined to be the sinister prelude to total war. Moreover, the calm was emphasized, at least in the countryside, by coincidence with one of the bitterest spells of winter weather within living memory.

For a few weeks Larkfield (as I have called the village) experienced something of that self-sufficiency which was the basis of English rural life in the days before Enclosure.

And now, as I write this introductory note, every vestige of that calm has been shattered. Larkfield watches the approach of happenings which have no equal in terror or frightfulness. And meanwhile spring unfolds with a completeness only matched by the completeness of the winter that preceded it: the English countryside puts forth her loveliest and best to front the enemy, like "a kneeling angel holding faith's front line."

Already the Larkfield I have tried to picture in these pages wears the aspect of a dream . . . but it is a dream that must be kept before our waking eyes when the horrors that sought to blind us are past. For it is from the ashes (if such must be) of the Larkfields of England that our phoenix strength shall rise.

England's might is still in her fields and villages, and though the whole weight of mechanized armies rolls over them to crush them, in the end they will triumph.

The best of England is a village.

May 1940   C. H. W.

CONTENTS

Chapter One	page 1
Chapter Two	21
Chapter Three	39
Chapter Four	51
Chapter Five	63
Chapter Six	79
Chapter Seven	99
Chapter Eight	117
Chapter Nine	131
Chapter Ten	145
Chapter Eleven	155
Chapter Twelve	173
Chapter Thirteen	191
Chapter Fourteen	209
Chapter Fifteen	225
Chapter Sixteen	237

ILLUSTRATIONS

The village under snow	frontispiece
Snowdrifts by the roadside	page 13
Telegraph pole	19
Promise of Spring	33
House martin	37
Timber and plaster in Essex	45
Harvest-bottle	49
A corner of an old barn	57
From any English hedgerow	69
Sheaf of oats	87
The end of the day	93
Pigeon-house	97
Children call them the Keys of Heaven	105
The village carpenter's handiwork	127
Essex cart	130
Coming home from the fields	135
Winnowing fan	144
The lane and the barn	149
Mutz	153
Wild Campion	165
Scythe in apple-tree	171
With glove and bill-hook	179
Mare and foal	189
Broken windmill under the stars	201
Corn dolly	208
By the mill-pool	217
Kneading trough	224
A flock of peewits	229
Rookery	235
The setting sun that brings the labourer home	247
Essex thatch	250
Signpost	251

Chapter One

I BEGIN this story of an English village in a wartime January that will be remembered in Larkfield as long as there are any of us alive to remember it and to talk of it. And it will not be of the war we shall speak. Indeed, during these last seven days, the war, for most of us, has been little more than a not very circumstantial rumour penetrating our homes by radio and (occasionally) by newspaper.

Not that, as a village, we are any more callous or unconcerned than other villages, but that, like most country people, our interest is mainly reserved for the things we understand, the things we know about by direct experience. War, for instance, first came home to us, as something that really had happened, when the telegram arrived announcing the death at sea of Mrs. Chayters' only son. Before the morning was out, everybody in the village knew of that telegram; and from that day onwards, U-boats, though none of us had ever seen one, were a dreadful reality—they had killed a man we knew and left a weeping mother in our midst.

But for a week now, war has been pushed into the background again by a much more immediate reality: the drama of its far-away happenings has been dwarfed by a much more actual drama here at home. Hardly an aeroplane has dared our skies for days. Even the soldiers from the neighbouring anti-aircraft camps have somehow been less in evidence. And although our volunteers still keep their punctual shifts at the local observation point, we have been too much engrossed in other things to give them the attention their patient service merits.

For days we have been almost cut off from the outside world—a community of some nine hundred souls huddled together in a white waste of snow. "Snowy Tuesday," some of the old folk say, recalling with peasant exactitude a bitter fall in 1881. Others call it "Black Tuesday." Snowy or black, however, we of a younger generation have hitherto been a little inclined to doubt their tales of outlying farms and cottages that were isolated for a week on end and of snow that drifted so high it was possible to walk over the tops of the hedges. Such things do not happen, here in the kindly south. So we said, and credited their tales to the proneness of old people for exaggerating the happenings of years gone by. Let them boast, it does no harm, anyway!

But now the same thing has happened in our own time. There *are* farms and cottages in the "uplands" (as we say, though nowhere hereabouts is more than three hundred feet above sea-level) that neither the baker nor the grocer nor even the postman can get near; and all around the village there *are* drifts of snow in the sunken lanes so high you can walk over the tops of the hedges. Thus humbled, we shall perhaps listen a little less incredulously in the future to the tales of our elders. And no doubt we, in our turn, shall seem as prone to the exaggerations of old age when we tell of the snows of this white January.

It is one of the merits of village life, as well as one of the penalties, that we are, even in the most propitious days, so closely interdependent one on another. And when such inclement weather as this shuts us away from the world, we are even more closely united. If there was kindness among us before, it is more than trebled now. If there was envy, hatred or malice, it seems for the moment to have been forgotten. Perhaps there is an element of fear compelling us to this unstinted kindness, a faint echo in us from the days when, to an extent not even the severest hardships can inspire to-day, men and women were forced to find safety in communal endeavour. Or perhaps it is nothing more than excitement, engendered by a spectacle in which, whether we will or no, we are all compelled to play our part. The same dead sky hangs over us all, day after day. The same snow comes flaking down on the just and the unjust alike. And the same uncanny silence fills us all, even to the most unsusceptible among us, with premonitions of we know not what.

Before the snow came, we used to be wakened in the morning by the sound of men going off to work. Voices below the Causeway told us that Tom Crutchly and Arthur Small were passing one another on their bicycles as they pedalled out of the village in the early dusk. "Nice mornin', Tom!" "Aye, it is that." And then silence again, broken only by the sound of the stream purling by the roadside. But once Tom and Arthur had gone by, punctual as the sun itself, others would soon follow.

It was amusing to lie abed, pleasantly half-awake, picking out the passers-by by the mere weight and rhythm of their tread. Easiest of all to recognize, of course, was Sam Merriman's, the blacksmith. At any time Sam shuffles rather than walks; but when he goes across to his forge, first thing in the morning, his heavy boots are still unlaced and then his usual shuffle would sound even sprightly by comparison. Kettle in hand, he ambles down the road to the forge, to boil some water for the morning cup of tea; and it is with this first unbuttoned appearance of Sam that the day really begins. His loud voice and his louder laughter, as he greets whoever comes along, are the cock-crow announcing the dawn, and any sounds and voices, earlier than his, are mere shy, hesitant bird-calls, timorously awaiting the master-herald of all. Sam has a word for everybody and everybody has a word for Sam; and those he does not meet in the road itself, he calls up to in their bedrooms: nobody is allowed to sleep on once Sam has appeared on the scene.

But now it is all quite different. No Tom or Arthur goes pedalling past, called from bed each morning for a pittance on some far-off farm. And when Sam does appear, the day is already so far advanced that nobody could rely on such a belated cock-crow. In that cold silence when the snow throws its first white light on to the ceiling, it is almost as if the end of the world had happened overnight, and, unaccountably, we were the only souls left alive in a blank and muffled world. At last, however, there are voices—voices unnaturally clear, and as it were suspended, because unaccompanied by the sound of passing feet, in a vacuum. And then, once we are up, we see what all the mystery is about. There is nothing the snow has not clung to and changed past all knowing. Roof and tree, road and garden, all have been fashioned anew in the night by a hand of miraculous cunning and to the whim of a mind that loves not colour.

And down by Mark Thurston's cottage, under the knot of elms we had thought so friendly and so familiar, half a dozen men have suddenly appeared from nowhere with a couple of horses and the village snow-plough. Monkish in their sacks, which they wear over their heads, the two corners tucked one into the other, the men handle the cumbersome implement that has lain on the grass by the roadside all the year, its massive shares decorated with cowslips in spring and hidden under a foam of kexes in summer. While some of them attend to the harnessing of the horses, others stand by, flinging their arms about like flails, in an attempt to stir some sort of warmth in their shivering bodies.

Whereupon, of course, Mark appears at his door, with not even a jacket to shield his seventy-seven years, and, what really is unusual, without his cap. No old farm-hand ever dreams of going about with his head uncovered, any more than he would dream of picking a bunch of wild flowers ("*them* ol' things: now if they was taters, I'd understand"), and so there is always a suggestion of nakedness in the sight of a hatless villager, his pale, unsunned brow contrasting so vividly with the remainder of his ruddy, weathered face. In Mark the oddness is emphasized this morning by the reflection of the snow on his high, shining forehead. With both hands thrust deep in his pockets, he watches the men struggling with their plough.

"Bless us, Bob," he says: "it's a rummy sort of furrer you'll draw this morning. And hadn't you better stick a twig o' something in Gipsy's forelock to keep them ol' flies away?"

But nobody takes any notice. Mark's little jokes are not always as keenly appreciated as he thinks they are; and anyway, the men are too cold this morning to pay attention to him. "Now then, Gipsy! Come up, Dimint!" And the hooded men follow their cumbersome plough up the road, cleaving a wide furrow through the snow that curls over and breaks, like the ploughed stubble in autumn. Mark turns away, shutting his door behind him.

For awhile yet the village maintains its empty silence. Double-thatched now, with straw and snow, the cottage roofs project their picturesque angles against the deadened sky. Over Goose End the ruined windmill flaunts its broken sails, set at Miller's Pride till they fall and ill able to support the weight of snow lodged on their upper edges. Gardens there are none, and every bush is a frozen fountain. Our meagre river, running through the centre of the village, is indistinguishable now from the Green that rims its banks. At other times, it alternates swiftly from a convenient mirror (beloved of photographers) for the reflection of the surrounding cottages to a muddy stench that causes the passers-by to pinch their noses in disgust; but to-day both mirror and stench are sealed in ice.

Buried somewhere beneath its white, unruffled surface are the inviting slides that traverse it from end to end—slides where the children of the village have enjoyed themselves as never since they were born and where even the farm-hands, returning from the fields in the early dusk, could not resist the temptation to drop their bicycles against the bridge and take a flying turn or two before they went home to tea. Later on, no doubt, somebody will brush the snow away, or at least enough of it to uncover the precious slides. But it will be beyond their power to restore the simple sport to the pitch of ecstasy it engendered all last week and the best part of the week before. For then there was a moon. And while the frost dropped silver stars on to the roofs and spun from every branch and twig a hoary lace that only the morning would discover, lads and girls, and children who should long ago have been abed, sped over the glassy river, wings at their heels, and filled the blacked-out village with their laughing voices.

The Green is the hub of the village and much admired by our visitors. Four roads intersect it, pale ribbons that cut the green grass into unacademic triangles; and the meeting-place of these four roads is a narrow brick bridge adequate enough for the trickle of water which, in summer, flows underneath it, but totally inadequate for the amount of traffic which such a convergence of roads must necessarily cause.

However, it is a charming bridge in its simple, unhistoric way, and the number of accidents its inadequacy has so far occasioned is not yet sufficiently impressive to stir our Parish Council to do anything about it. Not that we have ever urged the Council to do anything about it. On the whole, we are a conservative people and (often quite justifiably) suspicious of innovations. Besides, from time immemorial the bridge has been the haunt of such old men as Mark, who, turned out of the pub before their argument has reached a satisfactory conclusion, may surely be allowed to lean somewhere and finish their talk in peace?

But now there is nobody leaning against the bridge. There is nobody anywhere. Then one by one people begin to appear. A door opens, and a woman wrapped up in a shawl tied over her head like a rabbit's ears picks her slow way across the Green; or another door opens, and a man with a broom makes a futile effort to brush back the snow that has heaped over his step, like Canute trying to push back the tide.

The two butchers' shops, apparently, do not deem it necessary to open this morning; and the grocer's shop, whatever activities may be going on inside, presents an obstinately inhospitable front.

Only the post office is open. For Miss Dickson, though nobody would guess it from her jocular manner and her warm-hearted concern for the welfare of all of us, is a Civil Servant, and the Civil Service allows no concessions, or few, to the whims and eccentricities of country behaviour in general. Snow or no snow, business must go on as usual in the post office—or as nearly usual as the circumstances will allow. For even in the post office punctuality has been nullified by this heaping snow. The mail-van has not yet managed to get through to the village, and the postmen, who dare not do the sensible thing and go home for a hot drink and a second breakfast, must make the best they can of an enforced idleness, kicking their heavy heels on the floor and flinging their arms about, till Miss Dickson's imperilled sweet-bottles rattle on the shelves and even she can hold them in good humour no longer.

Nor is it only the postmen who are a little ruffled in temper by this unaccommodating weather. Tradesmen, tired of running their cars up roads that lead nowhere but to a blank wall of snow, are all inclined to be a little brusque these days. And as the first novelty wears off, even the farm-hands, stolid enough as a rule, are getting weary of being sent so far afield, spade in hand, to help the unemployed dig away the drifts.

Only in Goose End is there no appreciable sign of petulence. And the cause of such geniality, of course, is Sam Merriman. For Sam all this is welcome holiday: no horses to shoe, no spare parts to mend, nothing to do but exactly what he chooses to do. And what he chooses to do is as nearly nothing as makes no difference. Late to rise, therefore, at last he comes out into the roadway, shuffling along and kicking up the powdery snow like a ten-year-old. Carrying his broom over his shoulder, he volunteers to sweep anybody's snow away for them; and what his endeavours lack in effectuality, they certainly make up for in jocularity.

"Now then, midear: what can I do for you?" And he begins brandishing his broom about, as if the gestures of a magician were what the heaped-up doorstep needs, and not good hard work.

"Did y'ever see the like? They say it's nigh as high as a haystack over by Gilbert's Rise, and goodness knows when they'll taste baker's bread agen over at Vetches."

Sam continues to pat the snow with his broom, then stops altogether and says:

"Could you keep warm last night, midear? I couldn't, nohows. I said to missus, 'This is a rum 'un, if ever there was one.' It *was* cold. And do you know what she remembered me of? Well, I'll tell you."

It is no kind of weather to stand on the doorstep listening to Sam's tales and so he is invited inside. "Just for a minute, then," he says, and brings his broom in with him. He sits on the chair nearest the door, where he always sits, because he must keep one eye on what is happening out in the roadway. The fact that the door is shut now makes no difference: this is his chair. He hangs his cap over his knee, a childlike smile spreads over his broad features, and his ample body sags at once into complete and solid silence. He says nothing.

And then, being asked what it was Mrs. Merriman had reminded him of in the night, "O aye," he says, "I was forgettin'. Well, it was a terrible cold night, not so many years ago—and I suppose the cold last night must have put mother in mind of it. We 'ad two little ol' pigs that time: proper little dears, they was. And it got so cold I said to the missus afore we went to bed, 'Whatever'll us do with them little pigs out there, mother? We can't leave 'em out there all night.' So I went an' fetched on 'em in, and we wrapped 'em up in flannel, and we took 'em to bed with us. Mother had one along o' she and I had t'other along o' me. When I woke up in the mornin', I couldn't see my little ol' pig nowheres; so I felt down in the bed-clothes, and there he was, dead as a nit! S'pose I must a-laid on 'im in the night. But mother, she'd got her's all right. Now what d'you think of that, eh?"

And as if there is now nothing else to stay for, Sam puts on his cap, takes his broom, and opens the door.

"That sky do look reg'ler full of it," he says. "I reckon us ain't seen the worst yet."

Sam is quite right. By noon the snow is falling again as fast as ever, only this time it is accompanied by a driving, searing north-easterly wind. In fact, to say it "falls" is quite inaccurate: it blows along, horizontal with the ground, so that men walking with their backs to it are completely snow-covered on one side and have hardly a flake to show on the other. Spectacular as the village itself is, the really exciting scenes are in the roads and fields outside. Half a mile away is a world away now, for there are several places where the snow-plough would be useless and where nobody has yet arrived to dig a way through. And even where the spade and shovel have been hard at work, leaving an abrupt wall of snow on either side of the road, this latest gale is closing the drifts over again.

I find myself fascinated (it is the exact word for it) by the mere action of this silent drift-formation. With the small snow blowing over the fields at I know not how many miles an hour, melting in my ears and on my eyebrows, I stand watching the deathly masonry being piled up before me. So many of the narrower roads and lanes about here are slightly sunken between the cornfields and, as I watch, it is easy to see how these fields are being all but denuded of the snow that is blown off them and deposited in the lanes. The high walls, chopped out by the spade, have long ago lost their angularity: a lean lip is being formed on top of them and grows fatter as I watch, till it hangs in an evil pout. Already the shelving snow protrudes a quarter of the way across the top of the tunnel, it grows every minute, and I can see that before evening the whole lane will be blocked up again. And how silently, intently, irrevocably, the building goes on!

The snow blinds me. The wind whines. I had forgotten the war, and even now it is not our war I think of, but the war in Finland, where men freeze to death as they stand, one clutching at the collar of his coat, another trying with one hand to staunch the wound in his stomach; and I almost think, as I watch the remorseless, evil activity of these millions upon millions of infinitesimal flakes, that perhaps I have come just a mite nearer the reality of their suffering.

And yet it is all so incredibly beautiful. English hedgerows, those gestures of largess so frowned upon by the efficient agriculturists of to-day, have never lacked for poets to sing the praises of their tangle of June roses, or their singing birds, or their autumn galaxy of berries; but I wonder to-day why no poet (at least that I know of) has sung the praises of their boughs garlanded with the January snows. Perhaps it is for sheer lack of words. At any rate, roses and birds and berries are child's play, when it comes to putting them down in words, in comparison with these extravagant waves and billows of snow that ride over the hedges just now. Where there were boughs and branches, there are now tethered clouds of snow, fantastic flounces of snow; and underneath, where the rabbit had its hole and must now sit cowering in a warmth that still is not warm enough to satisfy his shrunken body, there are blue-mouthed caverns more mysterious even than those where the sacred river Alph ran "down to a sunless sea."

The cold sings in my head and reluctantly I return to the village. Though the snow is deeper now, and the wind colder, there are more people about. Somebody has brushed away the snow from the slides on the river, and a follow-my-leader trail of children, the girls shrieking and the boys expertly silent, skims from one end to the other. Young blood is easily roused and these heady children are much too absorbed in the new-found pleasures that every day provides now to stop and consider its possible uniqueness in their lives.

Very different is the attitude of some of the bunched-up adults, picking their dangerous way from this shop to that, panic-driven to store up while they may food against even worse days. Food, however, is not half so urgent or difficult a problem for us as water.

It is one of the lesser ironies of progress that, while we have electric light in the village, a radio set in every cottage and 'buses

Snowdrifts by the roadside

four or five times a day to take us the eleven miles between here and the nearest town, we are still dependent upon pump and stream for our water. Most of us, at least for the greater part of the year, prefer it so. We cannot see why on earth we should pay for water, when all we need do is dip a bucketful out of the stream or take a few turns at the pump. It stands to reason, we say, that water which has travelled miles through "the Company's" pipes cannot possibly be as good as water pumped straight out of the clean earth. We count for nothing the handiness of being able to turn on a tap and have your water ready to hand. And why should we, when gathering round the pump, pail in hand, is such a pleasurable occupation and so prodigal of friendly gossip? Summer evenings would not be half so enchanting if we could not saunter down to the pump and fritter away in talk of this and that the last, easy minutes of a heavy day. And I know that, for myself, if I were asked to name one of the most pleasantly characteristic country sounds, I should say the lazy, monotonous squeak of the pump handle in the hot dusk of the summer night.

But just now all the village pumps are frozen—and have been for days. On being informed of our predicament, the Council sent out orders to Mr. Peck to unfreeze the wells. But Mr. Peck was engaged on other jobs and so did nothing about it. Even in the best weather, eleven miles is a fairly safe distance away, and now, with the roads almost impassable, it is perfectly safe: no sanitary officer is likely to come prowling around to-day. So Mr. Peck, who is himself so often at the mercy of those in high places, uses his advantage and obstinately keeps us waiting. Even if he did crack the cement round the wells and apply his blow-lamp, he knows the chances are that the pumps will be frozen again to-morrow: then why not let them wait until to-morrow anyway? So, I suspect, he argues; and every hour we make the slippery journey across to our particular pump in vain.

However, it's an ill wind. . . . And I am glad that the one to benefit this time is Widow Fields. By some miracle of Providence, that would seem after all to have a special care for poor widows, Mrs. Fields' pump has remained unfrozen. Revealing an unexpected commercial acumen, she therefore charges one penny a pailful and prodigally sets a limit to nobody. Mr. Peck's obstinacy is her advantage; and I confess I find it hard to believe her when she cocks a sad eye up at the skies and says, "Well, I *do* think it's about time it stopped freezing now."

In the tap-room of the Wheatsheaf, some half-dozen men, old and young, are savouring their precious midday respite over a mug of beer. Mark is among them and speaks for the older generations: not so much by general consent, maybe, as by force of character. For one thing, words come easily to Mark and so he invariably gets in first. Then there is Luke Negus—a lad more useful with the tractor than the horse, but none the less a genuine countryman for that. He speaks for the younger generation.

Just now Mark and Luke (I know the juxtaposition sounds incredible, but such it is; and anyway, the only apostolic thing about them is their names) are sponsoring a conversation that has somehow evolved itself into a sort of impromptu game.

"And how do you tell a fox's track?" asks Luke, posing a query on behalf of the lads sitting at the same trestle-table with him.

"That's easy," comes Mark's ready response: "a fox has got five pads an' his tracks follow one another in a single line."

Score one for the old men.

And then: "Can you tell where a rat's been in the snow?"

It is the young men's turn to show their detective skill. "It allus drags its tail," says one of Luke's company: "it leaves a line between the footprints."

Score one for the young men.

"What is it, then," asks Mark, "as leaves a lot o' convicts' arrows wherever it goos? And all in a single straight line."

Everybody seems to know this one, probably because there is nobody here who has not gone beating with the Squire's shooting-party at some time or another.

"Pheasant," says one. "Partridge," says another. And the score is equal on both sides.

Thus the game continues: the badger with its four pads in a double line, the stoat with its two-by-two dimples ("ever so pretty it looks, going straight across the snow," says Luke), and so on, until suddenly, unexpectedly, the sport has played itself out, and, before anybody knows how or why, we are all listening to Ben Tetlow's account of how he, and a lot more men, forty-nine years ago, took days digging through the snow-drifts that filled the sunken lane over Gilbert's Rise: "'Tweren't no hill at all then," says old Ben, not a little surprised to find himself suddenly the focus of the company, "only one great big ol' lump of snow. We weren't short of wukk that winter, I can tell 'ee. And you may say it's nasty, heavy ol' wukk clearing away the snow; but it's a lot better'n doing a day with the stick-an'-a-half—that's what we used to call the flail," he adds, for the benefit of the ignorant youths of to-day. "I tell you, you don't know what wukk is, not these 'ere days."

"Come on, boys," says Luke, "let's get on with our job. I don't know whether it's what Ben would call wukk, but I reckon it's got to be done. Come on." They file out into the snow, leaving Mark and Ben to enjoy the fruits of victory.

"Just one more drink," says Mark, as the grandfather clock wheezes in the corner, preparatory to striking two: "I *think* there's time."

Ben has much more to say yet; and although the audience for whose special ears it was intended has gone away, he talks on. Mainly he talks to himself now, for neither Mark nor any of his cronies seems to be interested: the merit of the old days and the old ways is to be able to talk about them, not to have to listen to others talking about them. And so Ben's undoubtedly interesting recitative gets lost at last, submerged in a general conversation (which Mark has manœuvred) about the damage the pigeons are doing, this bitter spell, in the gardens.

And yet, as I come away from the Wheatsheaf into the silent, one-toned village, some of Ben's words still remain obstinately in my mind.

"We had to do pretty nigh everything for ourselves, then," he had said. "And for why? Because there weren't nobody to do it for us."

"And if we couldn't have done it for ourselves," he might have added, "we should have gone under." Perhaps that is one of the best things this snowy isolation has done for us: it has put all of us on our mettle—we are learning to do things for ourselves. And those things we cannot do for ourselves, we are learning to do without. In a minute degree, Larkfield recently has been more like a village used to be, I suppose, in the days before it began to ape (not very successfully) the towns. In the days before the windmill was a curiosity. In the days before radio and electric light and tinned food encouraged dependence. Old men such as Mark or Ben remember something of such days. Not much—but at least the sad afterglow of the self-supporting village. But for Luke and his friends, indeed for all of us under fifty, the village as a self-contained unity, baking its own bread from its own wheat, curing its own ailments from herbs gathered in its own hedgerows, is a fact out of history-books. And I cannot help thinking it is something of a pity that it should be so. Our newspapers don't arrive and we are vexed at their non-appearance. Our radio sets give out and we rush to the garage for a new accumulator. And we don't even like walking in the dark streets without a torch to show us the way. Are all these things so considerable an addition to our freedom, I wonder, that we ought not to count as loss the lack of self-reliance we have paid for them?

But for the snow it would be already dark. These are topsy-turvy days anyway, and the sky shines under our feet. And it is apparently a better sky than the one that normally should shine over our heads, for twilight will linger on an hour beyond its time, loath to leave a world so lovely. And so empty. Not a single cart has risked the roads all day. Even the motor-cars have consisted of little more than the milkman and the baker and such as were compelled, by a strange mixture of profit and duty, to go as far afield as they could. Now they too are home.

For once the pedestrian has the village to himself—a pleasure bestowed just when he is most unwilling to avail himself of it. A few cautious stragglers shuffle along the Causeway, and I have to scan their faces (for overcoats have suddenly appeared on bodies that never wore them before) to see who they are. But white masks are all I see; till "Good night to 'ee: good night!" proclaims the persons who wear them.

Chapter Two

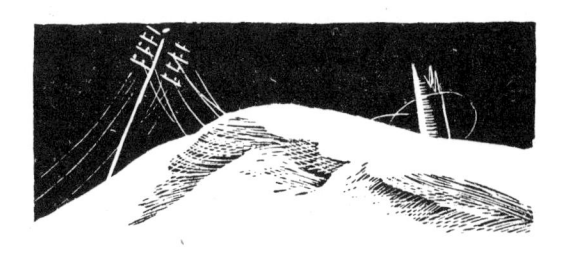

BENEATH the snow, that regiments everything into a uniform prettiness, the houses of Larkfield are as various and individual as the men who, down four centuries or more, have built them. They range from half-timbered cottages, neatly capped with straw thatch, to council houses, whose staring brick uniformity is a sorry indictment of this year of grace, nineteen hundred and forty. The former, even where their owners have neglected them, wear their age with dignity; but the latter have been ignominiously pushed out of sight, as if their approvers knew beforehand how rapidly (despite restrictions which, as one tenant put it, "don't even let you go to the privy in peace") they must deteriorate into a slum.

Every local style is represented in the architecture of Larkfield: from the Congregational chapel, with its Dutch façade hinting of the Flemish weavers who came over to enrich East Anglia with their craft, to the church, with its dog-toothed Norman doorway reminding us of those armoured knights who were our last and most considerable conquerors; from the steeply gabled butcher's shop by the Green, whose clustered chimneys crown as fair a piece of Tudor building as any round about, to the scores of four-roomed cottages under whose thatch generations of farm-hands have each night forgotten in sleep the ache and poverty of the day.

Thatch, in fact, is our special pride—though you would see no cause for pride just now, while snow, that other leveller, lays an equal pall on straw and tile alike. And well may thatch be our special pride, for this village lies in one of the richest corn-belts of the country: seen from an aeroplane, or even from the top of the church tower, Larkfield is a picturesque hotch-potch of angular roofs bundled together in a wide expanse of cornfields. Thatch is as apt to us here as limestone tiles to the Cotswolds; and although perhaps it is on the decrease to-day, it is still our most predominant roofing. Wherefore I find it strange that, in an 1848 directory of the locality ("under a lucid arrangement of subjects") the list of Larkfield craftsmen contains no mention of a thatcher. Four blacksmiths, yes, and two wheelwrights; a saddler and seven shoemakers (how the clay tugs a man's boots to pieces!); a cooper, a glazier, and even a "machine-owner"; but no thatcher. To-day there are two thatchers resident in the parish; and the Squire, whose many tenant-farms, I suppose, make him impatient of their well-known procrastination, has imported a third from Bedfordshire.

All craftsmen are notoriously independent: if they are not allowed to do a thing in their own time, they certainly will not do it in anybody else's. Their own satisfaction is the clock they work by; and you may as well try to make your garden plants blossom before they are ready as try to force the pace of a true craftsman.

So it is with thatchers. November gales may blow your roof off, and leave you to sleep beneath the stars; but Thatcher Wright will not come to your aid until he thinks fit to do so.

You walk out to his cottage and attempt to stir his pity with a recital of the plight you are in. "Ah, I dare say," is all he says: "there's everlastin' o' folk been after me these days. Dunno when I *shall* get round to you."

Exasperation dies down, and you even get used to sleeping under the stars. And then, one morning, when you had given up bothering any more, a load of straw arrives from somewhere and is shot down in your garden. It blocks the view, but there is a compensation: your rooms glow with a golden light. Then Wright himself arrives, crippled with the Old Man (as he calls his rheumatism), a bundle of spics and uncut hazels under his arm and a few tools tied on to his bicycle.

From that moment your house is a centre of attraction in the village. Perched on his ladder, with his game leg stuck out over the gables at so precarious an angle that your heart almost misses a beat to see him, he is greeted by everybody who passes; and although he always has something to say in return (usually sardonic), I have never yet seen him pause and turn from his work to see whom he was addressing.

In the days before the towns drained the blood away from the villages (offering errand-boys higher wages than farm-hands could earn) every thatcher had his assistant, whose job it was to draw the straw, cut the spics, load the yealms in the greip, and in fact do anything that might prevent the thatcher from wasting time by going up and down the ladder. Wright, in common with most other thatchers of to-day, has no recognized assistant. But he has three handsome, stalwart daughters. And sometimes, when the Old Man gets too "opstropulous" (as he says) he will bring his favourite daughter along with him: a silent, hefty girl with a head of fly-away hair as golden as new straw in sunlight. Expertly she trims the hazels and combs the straw; and as Wright calls to her from the ridge, where he sits in the sun shearing the scalloped pattern that runs from gable-tip to gable-tip, like a shepherd astride some monstrous golden-fleeced sheep at shearing-time, I think he sometimes wishes she had been born a boy.

It is, I know, a matter of some envy with him that Fremlin, his rival thatcher in the parish, has a son to assist him. True, Albert is more witty (in a bucolic way) than helpful. He spends most of his time, while his father gets on with the job, mimicking the more outstanding of our very mimickable community. Or, if it is not people, then it is birds and animals. Somebody in the village has heard the cuckoo—ten days, as every native knows, before he is due to arrive: it is only Albert. Or somebody's cockerel develops an unusual exuberance and crows throughout the livelong day: it is only Albert.

"A fool of a fellow, if ever there was one," says Wright, in no position to appreciate such homespun talent. All the same, he is probably thinking what a pity his own assistant can't be called Albert.

So the thatch grows. Always providing, of course, a wind does not intervene. No thatcher will work in a wind. Perhaps he has secured all the yealms in place, and nothing remains to do but the finishing-off—the straw to be trimmed round the eaves and over the dormer windows, the withy pattern to be woven along the ridge and gables, and so on; but as long as the wind lasts, the thatch must wait. The straw hangs over the windows, tousled as a beggar-boy's fringe; and every time the door is opened, another handful of straw-ends blows across the room.

But at last the thatch gets finished somehow, and Wright ties his tools on to his bicycle, flings a straight leg over the saddle, and disappears, leaving behind him a litter of hazel-chips and a garden where every plant grows straw.

How dandy the house looks now! Time, and the weather, will draw the gold out of the thatch and mellow it to a basic grey, as various as the light that falls upon it, rose at sunset, pink at dawn, moody as the sun and rain themselves. But just now—there it is: a new toy for all the village to pause and admire: an invitation to every homeless sparrow in the neighbourhood.

Or will it prove to have been an invitation to the martins, instead? For my part, that is what I sincerely hope. Two years, now, the martins have tried their best to bring up a family under the shelter of my eaves, and two years they have been routed. Will they try again?

It is not only that almost every other house in the village has its quota, and more than its quota in some cases, of the "lov'd masonry" of this favourite bird: but that to have martins building under your thatch is to have money coming into your house—and who so unworldly as not to enjoy the prospect of that? What should have given rise to the sentiment that one bird brings good luck and another ill, who knows?

"Have you ever seen a white blackbird?" Jim Adams asked me the other week, pausing, axe in hand, where he was felling an ancient ash. "If ever I see another," he went on, "I shall shoot it."

For all his bushy black brows and his gipsy eyes, Jim is a mild young man at heart, and so I was a little astonished at the amount of ferocity he put into his words.

"Why, Jim?" I asked.

"Because they bring nothing but what's bad," he replied.

From the story that followed, it appeared that a white blackbird had made itself very much at home in the cottage (now pulled down) where Jim lived with his busy young wife and his nigger-haired little girl.

"I suppose our Dot made a fuss of it," said Jim. "It was always in and out of the place. You couldn't keep it away with a broom."

Then Jim's young wife fell ill. The next he heard of the white blackbird was at Mrs. Rugby's. She had to be taken off to hospital. Then it appeared over at Joe Ferring's; and he fell off a load of straw and nearly broke his neck. So the tale went on: wherever the unlucky bird made its home, tragedy invariably accompanied it.

"Yes," said Jim, "if ever I see another I'll shoot it," and he brought his axe clean down upon the wound of the ash-tree, as if in emphasis of his intention.

Poor blackbird! "White as sin (as Andrew Young says) to your black kith and kin"—and to some countrymen as well, to judge by Jim's sad experiences.

But to return to my house martins. It was two years ago last May they made their first attempt to build under my eaves. I had watched other martins in the village, by hundreds, nesting and mating and scurrying round the houses, filling the summer heat with a twittering sound as of far-off water; and—I admit it—I was jealous. Why not *my* eaves? And then one morning there was a whirling and flashing past my window, like blown snow-flakes, and an incessant small bickering. The martins had arrived! I went outside to see. Already the work of building had begun. Close by one of the projecting joists of the roof, on the east side of the house (where certainly the air is not "delicate," as Banquo observed it should be), several dark mud-blots showed where the martins had secured the plinths and main uprights of their nest.

Most of that morning I spent watching the birds at their incredible task. By noon, however, they had little more to show for all their efforts than when I first caught sight of them. I think it is Coward who notes that a certain amount of play and aerial courtship invariably accompanies the initial stages of building: there was certainly much more play than work going on that morning. They would flurry in and out of the eaves, brushing past the wall in narrow arcs, twittering ceaselessly; and then, unexpectedly, one would settle. With her arrowy tail sucked tightly against the plaster, she turned her head this way and that, as she clung there, watching the brief assaults of her lover, and often her body would be so curved that beak and tail-tip made a complete half-moon against the wall. If the male bird managed to keep away long enough at a time, she would make a momentary effort to get a little work done, jabbing the clot of mud with her beak, kneading it in, and busying herself as a good housewife should. But her endeavours never lasted for long. Soon her companion would return, swooping up to her side with little *tchucks* of annoyance, as if he were luring her away. Come, time enough for house-building to-morrow!

That was in early May, when the celandines shone in the ditches and brimstone butterflies drifted like petals from the budding boughs. Once the martins got down to work in earnest, the nest was soon completed—a work to match the Pyramids themselves in cunning and audacity. It was a grand welcome-home, those days, to see, just above my door, a white-throated martin looking down at me with bright, intentful eye. I grew accustomed to the sibilant, soft music of those birds, as they flashed past the window and they gradually became the essential focus of that spring in my garden.

Then June took me away and the house was left empty. And when I returned in July, I knew at once that something was wrong. Martins, by the dozen, flickered over the roof and ransacked the evening sky for food; but they were not my martins; or, at least, they had nothing to do with the nest over my door. At first I thought perhaps the birds had hatched their eggs and the fledglings had already flown; but when I looked at other nests, in near-by eaves, where the martins had been busily building long before mine came on the scene, I was convinced that this could not be so —for there the youngsters were still thrusting their yellow gapes out of the nest-hole, clamorous for food and yet more food.

It was a straw sticking out of my martins' nest that first betrayed the truth. And then a sparrow-face appeared at the opening, chirruped saucily and disappeared inside again.

I know there are people who have a special affection for sparrows: they are so impudently indomitable, thriving where more delicate birds would perish, insouciant, undeniable, the *gamin* of the skies. Well, I give them all that and more; but still I do not like them. And if I did not like them before, how shall I like them now, when they have turned my martins out of house and home? My thatch had been wired to keep them away; but no, that did not defeat them. Those sparrows were determined to be my guests. If they could not get into the thatch, at least they could turn the martins out of their nest and make themselves at home there. Anyway, who *are* these fanciful weaklings that must needs hurry off south directly the cold weather comes? Come along, we'll show them who's master here: the nasty foreigners!

And so—well, the long and the short of it was that that cheeky face peeping out of my martins' nest made me see red. Saint Francis, who loved the house-sparrow equally with the nightingale, forgive me: I took a pole and poked the nest, till it fell in broken shards to the ground. That will teach you, I said; though of course it didn't.

Next morning the impossible seemed to have happened. My

martins were returning! The same swooping up under the eaves, the same soft chuckling as of a hidden burn, the same giddy spiral flights past my window. Then they would cling against the plaster, probing with their needle-beaks the ruins of their home. The sun shone on the pansy-blue of their backs, and breast and throat gleamed like snow. Their long, tapering wings were crossed above them, like the slim, folded wings of Fra Angelico's angels. And they chattered unceasingly. Out of the blue sky more martins appeared and joined them, pricking the morning with a multitude of small cries, glissading down the air and briefly inspecting the ruins as they passed. It seemed as if my martins had called all their friends and neighbours to come and help them to decide the momentous question whether, even at this late stage, they should build a second house and rear a second family. What finally decided them, I do not know; but after that one morning of frenzied consultation, they never came near the place again.

Next year, the same thing happened. With the celandines came the martins. A few feet away from last year's sad reminder, they built another nest. Again there was the bright eye looking out at me every time I passed. Again I was called away. And again the ragamuffin sparrows turned them out. So now I am wondering will the martins give me a third chance to get rich? Will they try again next spring?

Next spring! But nobody dares to think of next spring and what the war may bring for us with the warmer weather and the lengthening light. Thanks be, then, for the respite of these shivering days that shut away the fear of what may be.

Meanwhile, the martins, whom the spring will bring, whatever else it takes away, are far over the seas, and our native birds must endure the rigours of a record English winter. Fluffed out to twice their size, they look well-fed enough; but in truth their crops are well-nigh empty. On the radio last night a bland announcer's voice might have been heard encouraging us to feed the birds. It was, he said, a form of war-work. If the birds died, the crops would suffer next summer and we should suffer too. How many right things, these topsy-turvy days, are done for wrong reasons! We must feed the birds, not for their sake, but for our own. Well, so long as the birds are fed, that, anyway, is something. And maybe a habit will be started that will not cease: in the end we may feed the birds for their own sakes.

That was the way we thought about another war-measure: the evacuation of children. Like most other villages, Larkfield had its sudden influx of children from the towns. In those warm, end-of-summer days, the village rang with unfamiliar voices. There were difficulties and disappointments. Two worlds suddenly clashed, and the impact, to say the least of it, was uncomfortable. But there was also hope of compensation. How country life would change these pale-faced children! It had taken a war to do it; but at least the heritage would not be wholly evil, if afterwards we could point to a regenerated youth. And as we watched the colour come into those children's cheeks, and saw their limbs grow stronger every day, we began to believe the end of slums was in sight after all.

But alas, things did not turn out like that in the least. As the weather grew worse, and the bombers failed to arrive, the children one by one drifted back to the towns. The villages were themselves again. And so were the slums. It would almost seem that lasting good cannot come accidently: straws, for all the proverbs, will not save drowning men.

And as with the children, so with the birds. Anyway, I know I much prefer Jim Adams's reason for feeding the birds. He does it because he likes to do it. He loves the birds. And so does his wife and his little curly-haired daughter. When spring comes ("the flower that always makes me feel best," says Jim, "is the snow-drop") father and daughter will walk round the hedges in the evening, when work is done, looking for nests. Back home again, Jim will empty some small egg from the peak of his cap, for Dot to add to her growing collection. "We never take more than one," Jim says, sternly; "and then only if we haven't got one like it at home." Well, I dare say the birds would allow him so much at least, if their memories could stretch back as far as this bitter winter and the scraps of food he put out for them in his garden.

Sometimes I have heard Jim spoken of in the village as "soft." There is no very serious criticism implied in the speakers' words, for they know well enough how good a worker Jim is on the land; and one farm-hand is always quick to appreciate in another the deep store of inherited (rather than acquired) knowledge that lies behind all the tasks of good husbandry, ploughing, sowing, stack-making, and so on. No, it is not any inherent inability in him that they deplore, but a tendency to indulge the poetic. Birds'-nesting is all very well for boys and wild-flower gathering for girls, but a married man should have done with such things.

I have noticed it is usually the younger men who imply this lack in Jim. The older men sit back and say nothing—as if they did not altogether agree but were compelled, out of timorousness and their own tendency towards a similar indulgence, to keep quiet.

It is, shall we say, an expression of the spirit of the times. The young countryman of to-day, though he goes to the cinema at most once a week and is still leagues away in thought and feeling from the young mechanic in the cities, has nevertheless become enough affected by the modern attitude to put on at least some of the hard, protective armour with which men and women seek to shield themselves to-day from the pain of too much feeling. The armour fits him ill, as yet; but with combine-harvesters in the field and electrically milked cows in the shed, he is gradually learning to wear it with more ease.

Jim, however, will never learn how to protect himself from his feelings. His vulnerability shines in his black eyes. Yet his critics are wrong to impute this tenderness in him to "softness." Like his own favourite snowdrop, that rears its fragile head through the ice, his strength is in the very nakedness with which he dares to bare himself.

Jim is, in fact, that increasingly rare person, the genuine young

Promise of Spring

countryman. There is a certain loneliness in him, a proud isolation, as a result. He would have been more at home with the farm-hands of fifty and sixty years ago. They would have felt as he feels. But now they are old and outmoded, and Jim must walk a good deal alone.

His sense of this isolation is perhaps revealed in his shyness in first conversations; but once contact has been made, the shyness falls away and you find yourself talking with one whose interest in the land is a living thing, a responsibility even, echoing back to the days when every countryman, however poor, was master of his own few acres, his own few strips. Owning nothing (scarcely a pig in the back garden) the farm-hand of to-day has no sense of responsibility to the land. And where there is no responsibility, there is no intimacy. No wonder Jim walks alone! Such an intimacy with the land is the very breath by which he lives. It explains that tendency to indulge the poetic which his fellows are inclined to deplore, that tenderness which is only another name for his sensibility to the living earth.

"I wouldn't work in a town for anything," I once heard him say. "Whatever you do there hasn't got any *life* in it. Here, everything has got life in it."

Jim is not ashamed of his sensibility to the living earth, any more than his forebears, far back, were ashamed of theirs. Indeed, daily, though perhaps unwittingly, he encourages a like sensibility in his child. To him a dunnock or hedge-sparrow is always a Hedge-Betty, a thrush is a Mavis, and a flower of the lesser bind-weed is a Hug-me-Tight; and in speaking their names so natively, he proclaims immediately his kinship with the long-dead men who christened the goldfinch King Harry, the owl Billy Wixey, and the harebell Our Lady's Thimble. Such names are a lot of nonsense to the majority of the modern generation of farm-hands. Standing there in their dungarees, by the side of their tractor, its oil spattered on their faces and its fumes caught in their hair, they would feel awkward to be heard speaking these old poetic metaphors.

How many times, for instance, in the Wheatsheaf, have I heard some old man (Jim's spiritual brother of fifty years ago) speak vivid, homespun words that have merely evoked a giggle from his young listeners.

"If you want to get your rights in this parish," said Mark, the other day, voicing one of his pet criticisms of the way things are to-day: "if you want to get your rights in this parish, you've got to be either crafty, or wicked, or a downright liar—and goo about lookin' like a farden kite with its tail blew off! Don't, nobody'll take a mite of notice of 'ee."

And all the response he got was: "Mark's a proper comic, so he is," the speaker's own language being as devoid of poetry as a marrow of meat.

In the diminished numbers of its genuinely responsible young farm-hands, however, Larkfield is no worse off than any other English village up and down the country. Possibly it is even a good deal better off than many. No railway runs through our village and the nearest town is eleven miles away. We have no cinema and we have no dance-hall. Several of us have never seen the sea, although it is only some twenty miles away. And Jim was not conscious of anything unusual in his confession to me one day that he had never seen a mountain: "I used to think they was like this," he said, moulding an imaginary single peak with his hands, "but I suppose I'm all wrong about that!"

The depth of a man's knowledge is not to be measured by the number of miles he has travelled—as every second tourist to-day bears witness. Travel broadens the mind, we are constantly being told; but there are some things better measured by depth than by breadth. And experience is one of them. Jim has never seen a mountain and old Mrs. Cook has never seen the sea; but the daily lives of both of them are an ample witness of the intensity of experience of which they are capable.

Our isolation, therefore, is not without its advantages. Among the older generation (for whom, still, all that is not Larkfield is foreign) it has preserved a goodly measure of that sense of responsibility to the land which was the very basis of our greatness half a century or so ago; and among the younger generation it has at least kept alive a more hopeful semblance of that responsibility (for all Jim's comparative loneliness to-day) than might otherwise have been the case. Some villages have not even their Jim.

And certainly we are fortunate in the number of old people still living among us, women like Ann Bright who brought up twelve children in a four-roomed cottage on wages that, at their best, never exceeded seventeen shillings, men like Mark Thurston who at seventy-seven are in possession of a vitality and an integrity that colour every word they say, to give an example to such as care to follow it.

Ann stands in her doorway taking the sun and watching the world go by. "Yes, I'm feeling as happy as all the birds!" she says. And she means it too. And, hearing her words, how can one not be glad to be living in Larkfield to-day?

Chapter Three

WHATEVER the villager makes of his church to-day, there it stands, towering over his cottage, as powerful in its masonry, if not in its appeal, as it was hundreds of years ago. He may seldom go inside it, but it is part of his life now, like an apple-tree in his garden that has been there ever since he was a boy. Perhaps he makes no more use of his church than as a clock. What's the time? and he opens his back door, cranes his neck, and reads the hour between his neighbours' thatches. Or he passes it every morning on his way to work, and there it is to greet him again on his return at night. Or he hears its bells blowing across the fields to him as he walks behind the drill.

"The wind's gone round to the west again," he will say, glad of the sound for its welcome news of coming rain.

Such usages may be secular, but may they not somehow serve more than a secular purpose? The mere fact of the church, so persuasively in evidence every day, telling the hour for him and prophesying the weather, perhaps helps to keep alive in him some echo of a faith more alert in earlier times. Willy-nilly, he is a child of the twentieth century, and the twentieth century is a faithless one; yet there is a possibility that faith will not wholly die in it, while church bells chime across the fields to tell the time of day.

In Larkfield to-day, as in most other villages, it is mainly the women who attend the church: they are more traditional than the men, more timorous of breaking with the past. And so it is upon them that the vicar chiefly relies for his meagre congregations and upon them that he spends the greater part of his clerical endeavours. Except maybe for a funeral, whether of a relative or some lifelong friend, the men rarely enter the church at all. They may still touch their caps to the vicar when they pass him in the street, but it is usually in obedience to a respect they learned (or, rather, had thrust upon them) when they were young: the ghost of an old habit instilled in the days when such deferences were compulsory.

"It were forced religion in them days," says Mark: "we '*ad* to goo to church. And if it wasn't parson as compelled us, it was Squire. But we got the better of 'em sometimes, for all that. We used to hang round the church porch a Sunday mornin', waitin' till Squire drove up in his carriage an' pair. 'Mornin', Thurston,' he'd say: 'mornin', Tetlow,' and time he'd gone inside and was kneeling down in his pew, we'd be on our way home agen, to set the taters, or somethin' like that."

Nowadays, relieved of compulsion, the men no longer even make pretence: they just stay at home altogether. Called upon to defend their attitude, they might very well make use of another of Thurston's remarks: "Religion ain't just goin' to church, now is it? It's how you live—leastways, that's how *I* see it."

Nevertheless, there is one occasion, apart from funerals (which anyway are attended perhaps as much out of deference to the dead as out of respect for the living) when men may be seen, in plenty, walking up the church path at the summons of the bell. "Harvest festival," I remember one non-churchgoing farm-hand saying to me: "harvest festival? That somehow ain't *like* church, not to say church, is it?" And the implication was, I imagine, that with the corn and the flowers all around him, the hearty singing and the rather more informal air of the whole service, he felt at his ease; and ease is a feeling few farm-hands associate with attendance at church.

At harvest festival the fields are brought inside. Everything a man's eye rests upon, then, is familiar. This is the corn he has tended all through the year, from green blades piercing the first fall of snow, to rustling ears swept down by the binder; these are the marrows and flowers and apples from gardens just like his own. No need for his thoughts to get mazed at the prospect of some frightening after-world, while there are these real and very familiar things all around him—Tom Clissold's potatoes, pride of the village allotments, Baker Swift's crisp brown loaves, and those shaggy dahlias, nursed so carefully all through the winter to blossom at last in his own back garden. The very smell of the church at such a time is comforting and friendly, a blend of all the scents that surround him at his work. Yes, it is all actual enough and close to every day. Why, somebody has even brought a dozen sugar-beet, and there they lie in a neat pyramid, chopped and scrubbed, to remind him (as if he would be likely to forget it!) how his fingers have ached with the cold, till he could almost have cried, and each boot has weighed a ton, as he stood out there in the bitter fields cleaning the roots of leaf and mud and pitching them up into the tumbril. "Harvest festival? Well, that somehow ain't *like* church, is it?"

So the majority of the men feel; but with the women it is rather different. The church necessarily occupies a larger place in their lives. Not only because they mainly comprise its congregation, but because, one way and another, it subtly controls several of their most considerable pastime activities. Such activities (like the Women's Institute that has become so firmly established in every village) may advertise themselves as strictly non-sectarian and non-political, but the theory is scarcely maintained in the practice.

It cannot very well be otherwise. The village women, it is decided, need entertaining, need educating, need organizing. Very well, and who else is there to do these things if not the women of the "leisured" classes? In every village there are the equivalent to the Squire's wife, the retired Colonel's wife, the Vicar's wife, the pensioned Anglo-Indian official's wife, and the elderly spinster daughters of some dwindled aristocrat: on these the work of entertaining the village women, educating and organizing them, is bound to fall. They have the time on their hands, they have the money, and quite often they have the genuine aptitude and inclination. But they are, almost without exception and by the very nature of things, Church of England and Conservative; and even with the very best intentions in the world, they cannot help colouring the organizations they control with the hues of the Church and Party they support.

Unfortunately, the Church and Party they support are largely propped up on the idea of class-distinction. However unintentionally, therefore, a suggestion (if no more) of condescension informs the activities of these leisured women on behalf of their presumedly inferior sisters. But their inferior sisters are no longer quite so uncritical of condescension as they used to be. Conservatism dies hard where the people live mainly on and by the land; but even the remotest villages, these days, are slowly shaking themselves free of every vestige of servility. Such condescension implies a denial of the villager's proper pride and he is quicker to defend that pride to-day than he was a quarter of a century or less ago.

"Is Sam at home?" the retired Anglo-Indian official inquires of the blacksmith's wife. "Mr. Merriman is over at the forge, sir," comes the prompt reply, dignified and without emphasis. The quiet rebuke is unmistakable.

On the other hand, Sam himself, the very next day, will lapse into something at least reminiscent of the old servility. The Squire, in one of whose cottages he lives, calls and asks him to give lodging for a few days to a timber-valuer who is coming down to assess some trees on the estate. Sam hates lodgers, because they are a severe restriction on that simple liberty which, at seventy, he has just managed to achieve. Nevertheless, he agrees. Afterwards, of course, he complains. "Then why did you say yes?" he is asked. "Well, I live under 'im, don't I?" he replies: "what else could I do?"

But in any case there is a difference here between Sam's lapse

Timber and plaster in Essex

into near-servility and his wife's quiet insistence on her pride: liberties taken by the Squire and liberties taken by the retired Anglo-Indian official are not at all one and the same thing. Merely by virtue of the long-standing position his family have occupied, the Squire is allowed to encroach at least an inch or so on Sam's liberty without giving undue offence: there is a bond between them, forged through long generations. But the Anglo-Indian official has no such tradition to sanction his assumption of intimacy.

Indeed, the Squire is in quite a privileged position. Perhaps, in this respect, Larkfield is more fortunate than some villages. Our Squire is not only Squire—and local Member of Parliament and Chairman of This and Manager of That—he is also farmer. Four thousand acres is the extent of his estate and it includes most of the major farms in the parish. Some of these farms are rented out, others are worked by foremen who live in a few rooms of the vast, half-timbered farm-houses put at their disposal; but one of them, the Home Farm, is the Squire's special pride—and the pride, also, of the whole parish.

Mention of this farm, and of the good husbandry practised on it, occurs in several old farming books; and Arthur Young himself wrote in praise of the methods employed on it by one of the Squire's ancestors. If you want to see ricks neatly trimmed as they were in the days when the farm-hand's "task" included a hundred and one little jobs neglected to-day for lack of time or inclination or ability, go to the rickyard of the Home Farm and see how the score of ricks there, some round, some oblong, some set on iron staddles, proudly proclaim the joy of a job well done. If you want to see a plough-man draw a straight furrow across half a mile of field, go to the Home Farm fields in autumn when the ploughmen rip open the long stetches in the stubble and leave them wavering across the undulating land like ribbons flicked out in the wind. And if you want to be assured that the "old-fashioned" farmer still exists, loving his land as he loves his wife, go and have a word with Mr. Saling, the Squire's Home Farm foreman. You will probably find him wandering round the fields somewhere, on his way from superintending one job to superintending another, and as you walk by his side you will notice how he continually steps a stride or so out of the way to dig up some dock or thistle (for his walking-stick is also his "spud") that his keen eye has seen while you have been talking.

And all this evidence of careful husbandry—Mr. Saling and his spud, the neatly trimmed ricks, and the straight furrows wasting so little at the headlands—is the Squire's pride, as it was his father's before him and as we all hope (not quite so confidently as we might wish, perhaps, for even the stoutest tradition is apt to snap these days) it will be his son's after him.

No wonder, therefore, if the Squire wins the respect of the village and is allowed a certain amount of licence even with Sam. It is generally claimed that the days of Squiredom are over; and goodness knows there are enough forsaken mansions up and down the country, their dead eyes staring across the ruined park, to give grounds for such a claim. But Arley Hall at least still stands intact among its fertile acres. Its Tudor brick façade, rosy as a peach under the rays of the setting sun, still maintains a gallant defence against the enemy. Progress makes no conquest there. In all its great length and breadth there is no bathroom, and the servants (hard to get and harder to keep) must each evening carry up dozens of oil-lamps from the kitchen.

Such obstinacy in the face of forward-moving time may seem crass or merely apathetic. Arley Hall belongs to the old order and it is just being wilful to pretend it doesn't. Maybe, we say; but we are not quite convinced. We do very well under the Squire and would be sorry to see him depart; and we certainly do not wish to see Arley Hall converted into some screaming girls' school. Squiredom, it seems to us, depends upon the Squire. It can be a good thing and it can be a bad thing. And if it is asking too much of poor human nature to count upon a sufficiency of good Squires to justify such a scheme, then we can only say that in Larkfield, at any rate, we are fortunate. Another Squire might make us think differently; but so long as the present one justifies his place in the grand tradition of his fathers, serving his land and the people who work on it, we are satisfied.

Yes, we do very well under our Squire, thank you; and some of us have seen quite enough of the way things work under the up-to-date, impersonal system that is prophesied for us not to prefer to be left alone. As countrymen and countrywomen we know the value of the personal as compared with the impersonal, and we willingly accept the possibilities of error that such an attitude entails. Our daily contact with growing things has taught us this much. While we may, therefore, let us keep our Squire, because at least he reminds us, in a world of increasing statistics and bureaucracies and government from afar, of a communal life based upon the discipline of personal relationship.

And let us also keep our church. For many of us it may be little more than a timepiece, a weather-glass, an imposing piece of architecture with a chilly and rather musty interior. But there it is —the most powerful reminder in all the village of that slow pyramid of life of which we are the insignificant apex.

The leaning tombstones in the churchyard are a salutary warning, each time we pass by them, of our own relative unimportance: the lowly mosses and the humble lichens are sufficient to blot out our names when we are gone.

Chapter Four

IF the church, then, is there to cater for our spiritual needs, the pub is there to cater for our bodily needs. The one undeniable and yet somehow remote; the other equally undeniable but not at all remote. Church and pub, spirit and body—and it is perhaps not without significance that whereas the one is mainly frequented by women, the other is mainly frequented by men. The village pub, indeed, is the farm-hand's club.

I should, of course, say "pubs," for in Larkfield there are four of them. And they flourish as the green bay-tree. It is true that my directory informs me that, in 1848, there were six pubs in the village; but what is the loss of two pubs in a hundred years?— particularly when it is recalled how large were men's thirsts in those days. A man took his ten-pint harvest-bottle with him into the fields and would have thought himself extraordinarily hard done by if the farmer did not supplement this with liberal supplies from his own farm-house brew.

To have retained four pubs out of six, therefore, is not too bad. And when I say they flourish, I particularly have in mind the Wheatsheaf, over against the village green. Some of us, more unprogressively minded than most, are inclined to think it has perhaps flourished too much of recent years. In the old days there were only two rooms and one of them was obviously not for use. Sometimes a stranger would make a mistake and open the wrong door, but a first glimpse of the sedate plush furniture inside and a first sniff of the uncirculated air were usually enough to make him hastily withdraw.

A pub should be entirely democratic, and nobody could have claimed that the Wheatsheaf was anything else in those days. We all used the same room, shared the same fire, sat on the same worn, shiny forms, and studied (if ever we were so unoccupied or bored as to notice them) the same battle-pictures and sale-bills on the wall. If we were disturbed by the fact that Mark spat liberally (and, it must be said, accurately) into the fire, only just missing our coat-sleeves as he did so, then the remedy was in our own hands—we could at least move out of range. And if Ben Tetlow became more garrulous than usual, or launched again on a yarn we had already heard more times than we could possibly count, well, it was a simple and effective antidote to invite him to a game of dominoes. Ben may not concentrate on many things, but one of them is certainly dominoes.

Now everything is changed. Instead of two rooms there are three; and all of them are for use. Furthermore (and perhaps this is the innovation we jibbed at most) all are labelled: Saloon Bar, Visitors' Room, and Tap Room. "It's as bad as the Army," I heard Mark say, as he stood watching the workmen painting the white lettering on the doors: "officers and their wives, men and their women."

Not that the labels were necessary. I cannot imagine Mark walking by mistake into the saloon bar, with its tile-topped tables and its satin cushions on the chairs. Rose-pink satin cushions are not Mark's idea of pub-comfort, and so he and his cronies sit round the trestle-tables in the tap-room in monkish simplicity, and no doubt in time they will feel just as much at home there as they did in their old den in the days before the renovation. As yet, even in the austere tap-room everything is still a little too new, too clean, too shiny. Mark, for instance, is not quite sure about spitting into the handsome new fireplace; and when, carried away by his own exuberance, he so far forgets himself as to do so, the action is invariably followed by a wrinkle of pained apology on his shiny forehead.

As for the visitors' room, I have no idea who uses this inner sanctum—if anybody does. When the alterations were first completed, Tom Clissold, our proud landlord, showed me over the building—the tap-room, the bar, the saloon, and then, with the air of a magician about to produce out of the hat the most astounding surprise of all, the visitors' room. He opened the door and I peered inside: to have entered would have been more than I dared and clearly more than Tom expected. But the brief view revealed such an assembly of new furniture and brilliant china vases, dyed pampas grass and brass fire-irons as immediately suggested the windows of a furnishing shop in the Tottenham Court Road. And I confess I still find something more than a little incongruous in the thought of that paint-plush room at the core of a Larkfield huddled under the simple stars.

Commercially considered, of course, Tom's improvements were made just in the nick of time. Hardly was the new paint dry on the doors, or the new bottles temptingly displayed above the bar, when war was declared. A couple of anti-aircraft units were dumped down in the neighbourhood and naturally the very first explorations of the soldiers led them straight into the Wheatsheaf. Tom's saloon bar has never been empty since. What was panic and almost pandemonium at first, settled down after a few weeks into a steady and profitable routine.

In fact, prosperity is in the very air at the Wheatsheaf these days, and Tom's smile grows with each succeeding week. Even this unprecedented weather has been to his advantage, for the camps are cold and the duty tedious, and inevitably the soldiers seek what solace they can find in the bottles and barrels of the Wheatsheaf. Some have brought their wives with them and some their friends, and as many of these as Tom's bedrooms will accommodate are now additional aids to his prosperity.

The military influx, moreover, has given Tom an importance over and above his status as landlord of our most considerable pub. Tongues, even soldiers' tongues, are set talking by good drink, and he can hardly help himself if, fulfilling his pleasant and profitable duties, he overhears a thing or two not perhaps meant for civilian ears. He knows; and of course we know that he knows—by mysterious nods and becks and hints he sees to that. But Tom is far too wise a man, and too patriotic an Englishman, to divulge what it is he knows. "A careless word may send thousands to their death": so reads the warning on his walls. Well, he at least will not be guilty of homicide. Maybe whatever he knows amounts to nothing that matters; but by keeping it to himself, at least he adds something to his stature. And remembering that gleaming visitors' room, I think perhaps he needed an additional cubit or two.

Only in the bare-boarded tap-room has the war so far made no appreciable difference. Perhaps it is because, as yet, so little has happened to bring the fact really home to us. Perhaps it is because the *habitués* of the Wheatsheaf do not fundamentally understand why there should be any need for anything to "happen." They understood the last war well enough, or at least they thought they did. Many of them took part in it—including Mark, who disguised his age and joined the Army Veterinary Corps. And if the War Memorial on the green outside the pub (defying history with its plain assertion that the war lasted from 1914 to 1919) no longer rouses any very pronounced feelings in them, at least they thought the struggle it commemorated was inevitable and righteous enough at the time.

It used to seem to me, in those fateful months preceding the actual declaration of war, one of the most hopeful signs of progress that nobody in the Wheatsheaf (or in any other village pub I chanced to walk into) ever showed anything but dislike at the prospect of another war. "If they want me, they'll have to fetch me this time," was the most frequently heard comment. Certain things began to

A corner of an old barn

be recalled: kindnesses met with from the enemy, lies told at home, and a vague conviction that, whatever might be the differences between one nation and another, they certainly did not justify the barbaric slaughter of war.

"I expect if you was to go over there," I remember Tom Clissold saying, who had never been beyond these shores, "you'd find them there Germans pretty much about the same as you an' me. Leastways, they're wonderful fond of their beer, I'm told, an' I reckon that counts for *somethin'*, don't it?"

In spite of increasing provocation, goodwill was still the characteristic attitude of the nameless thousands that make up the Larkfields of England. War could not happen again.

But it did. And gradually I noticed a change in the men's attitude. Instead of "If they want me, they'll have to fetch me," now it was, "Well, I suppose I'll have to go." No enthusiasm, no conviction: merely a dull acquiescence in the inevitable.

And in spite of the obvious barbarities of the enemy abroad and the persistent propaganda of the authorities at home, this is still very much the attitude to-day. Not that the men talk a lot about the war. An illustrated daily paper lies on the table, shouting some new sensation from its two-inch headlines; but few bother to pick it up and read it. The voices of the soldiers in the saloon bar drift round the corner; but we cannot see the khaki, and the stray words sound peaceful enough. So our conversation follows the course all country conversation invariably follows: the weather, the crops, the new tenants over at Vetches, and local matters in general. Sometimes a concession is made in favour of matters of more national import, such as the ill-management of "this 'ere rashoning business" or the scarcity of pig- and chicken-food ("They tell us we've all got to keep a pig in the sty," says Luke Negus, "but they don't tell us what we're goin' to feed 'em on"), but even such national matters are only viewed from a purely local viewpoint.

It would be difficult for a stranger to tell, from the average conversation in the tap-room of the Wheatsheaf, that we are at war. These men are incorrigibly peaceful. The land is their whole life; and war, until it enters their very homes, remains essentially a secondary consideration with them.

How different, for instance, is their attitude to the black-out, compared to the attitude of their brothers in the towns. Perhaps Mark Thurston's comment, the other day, sums up as well as any the general reaction of such born-and-bred countrymen.

"I don't like it," he said, "and I shall be wholly glad to see the back of it. When my missus has got into bed, I like to slip back the curtains, so's I can lie and look outside, time I ain't asleep. I like to see the moon through the window, and my ol' tree, and a little owl a-sittin' on it—whoo-ee! whoo-ee! That's being alive, that is; but this 'ere's like being dead. You might just as well be in your coffin."

Smart as the Wheatsheaf is, and admirable its service, there are nevertheless times when my loyalty to Tom wavers and I find myself gravitating towards another pub on the edge of the village. Inevitably a pub takes its colour from those who regularly frequent it. It is their club and owes its character to their many tics and foibles. But sometimes even the tics and foibles of Mark and Ben and the rest are powerless to resist the imposition of an alien character on the Wheatsheaf. Usually this only happens at week-ends and in summer. Then our tidy (but never too tidy) green is all but obliterated with motor-cars and picnic-parties, and the Wheatsheaf is crowded to the doors with young men and women who have come out into the country for the day. The Wheatsheaf's regular customers are silenced before such a happy, voluble crowd. Indeed, they are hardly visible. And at such times it seems only courteous to clear out of the way altogether and leave our guests to the unimpeded enjoyment of their visit. To-morrow we will return and clear up after them; but to-day we will leave them in full possession —in fact, there is no alternative.

On such occasions, therefore, I quit the urbanized atmosphere of the Wheatsheaf and take my drink at the Three Horseshoes.

There will be no crowd there (Harry Clark, the landlord, would not know how to deal with it if there were), and every voice will have a familiar tone about it and every word a native twist.

The Three Horseshoes is less a house than a honeycomb: to draw a plan of its oddly shaped cells and passages, every one on a different level from the other, would be quite beyond my power. One thing these cells and passages have in common, however, and that is a certain severity. There are no rose-satin cushions in the Three Horseshoes; nothing but good, honest wood. And there is nothing progressive about Harry. He is only half, perhaps only a quarter, the landlord of the Three Horseshoes; the rest of him is a blacksmith. And when, in his own good time, he comes to bring you your beer, he brings quite a lot of his forge in with it. The yellow end of a home-made cigarette (constantly being lit and as constantly going out again) hangs from his lower lip; soot colours the rest of his face and his lithe, strong arms; and instead of a barman's apron he wears a bit of old leather, cut to ribbons and seared with fire.

In fact, the landlord of the Three Horseshoes has always been half that and half something else; and one of Harry's predecessors has left behind him a local reputation which, however skilled a craftsman he may be, the very nature of the times will deny to Harry himself. Many a craftsman, dead and buried these fifty years or more, still keeps his memory green in the village by some work of his agile hands—a field-gate here, good for another quarter of a century, a neat piece of house-thatching there, or even a scrolled latch in some out-of-the-way cottage window where mass-production frames have not yet been introduced. And so the memory of Natt Witherby the cooper still lives on, kept green by those oaken harvest-bottles (kegs, as some call them, or costrels) of which he was the master-maker in the locality.

Not that many of Natt's harvest-bottles are still to be seen. Here and there you may find one hanging on a rusty nail in some cottage outhouse, its iron hoops falling away, its paint weathered or gone altogether, and its leather handle and trimly shaped vent-pegs as irretrievably lost as the dark, shining bullock's horn from which its owner drank his beer in the harvest field. But for the most part, Natt's bottles have been broken up and burned, and Natt is remembered less by the sight of them than by the reputation they earned in years gone by.

Harry may have all of Natt's skill in those strong hands of his, but he has to spend it on such severely circumscribed jobs as the mending of stoves and grates, the riveting of cart-wheels, and the patching-up of factory products which the craftsman in him abhors. His fate is the fate of most village blacksmiths to-day, but at least he is more fortunate than most in having his little pub to fall back on. His customers may not be many or very profitable; but they are his friends. All the week they must more or less look after themselves and be content with only an occasional visit from Harry, who stumbles in from the forge for a moment just to see how things are going.

But on Saturday night, washed clean of soot and with a whole cigarette between his lips, he is a host in a hundred. It will be strange if Ned Freeman is not there with his accordion, and many a forgotten country song comes to life over the glasses of beer. And even after closing-time, when his customers should all be gone, Harry sits on in the cloudy tap-room, discussing the mysteries of life with a few chosen cronies.

"No, Jim, you don't want to go home yet awhile. Drat the missus! I should a-thought you had enough of her jaw all the week. Why, I'm only just beginnin' to wake up! Did you see that bit in the paper the other day. . . ."

But Jim resists the lure of the landlord's intriguing conversation and goes home. And Harry is left alone, dreaming while the last embers fade.

Chapter Five

A S I look out on the snow, dinted only with the feet of birds, I think that if there is one person in Larkfield whom it must please, more than another, that person is surely Charlie Beslyn. (Sam I leave out of count. Almost everything pleases Sam, providing he is in the mood.) More than once I have heard Charlie Beslyn complain at the fleeting nature of the English snow, no sooner come than gone again.

"It always used to rile me, when I was a nipper," he said, "because I never could get up in time to see the snow before somebody or something had spoiled it."

To see the snow before the dirt had smutched it, however little, was Charlie's boyish ideal, and somehow he never could manage it. The poet in him, even then, longed for perfection, complete and entire, and it "riled" him that perfection should always remain just beyond his reach.

Well, if unsmutched snow is still his symbol of perfection, he has had plenty of opportunities to see it lately. Charlie lives about half a mile outside the village, and every field he can see from his windows now must be covered from hedge to hedge with pure, driven snow. No need to get up at dawn, lest somebody's nailed boots should spoil it before he can enjoy it: all day, and day after day, it keeps its white perfection. Charlie should be happy now.

I had known him a long time before I learned that he was a

poet. Perhaps I should have guessed. That he was no ordinary farm-labourer was clear enough at the very first glance. Lean-cheeked and unshaven, he looked at me with black eyes of diamond brightness. Those eyes were keen and missed nothing, and their brightness was perhaps less of laughter than of avidity—an avidity to drain the honey out of every moment, every thing. His hair (I have never seen him wear a hat and that alone sets him apart from his fellow-countrymen) was inextricably tangled over a high-domed forehead that later reminded me of another rural poet, though immeasurably his peer—John Clare, "the Peasant Poet of Northamptonshire."

I first got to know Charlie, however, through casual conversation, as a middle-aged countryman who "farmed" his garden, and lived with his sister in a thatched and tiled cottage outside the village. Indeed, our conversation in those days was nearly always confined to the garden; and yet, even then, there were hints in his words, gleams of a muddled mysticism, flashes of original thinking, that set him apart from other men. Even his attitude to his garden was original and quite unlike the strictly utilitarian attitude of most cottagers. Its crowded acre combined beauty and use in a most unusual way. Flowers and vegetables grew together, dahlias bloomed among the cabbages, the foot-long tassels of Love-lies-bleeding trailed over the turnips, roses climbed the apple-trees, and giant sunflowers of incredible diameter peered with phoebus-faces here, there and everywhere.

If there was order in Charlie's garden, and I believe there was, it was an order devised entirely by himself to please his own individual whim. He has an old wireless set and, for all I know, may listen regularly to the comfortable voice of Mr. C. H. Middleton; but if he does, it is certainly with no slavish intention to follow that omniscient gardener's advice. In gardening as in everything else, Charlie obeys his own laws. He will give you, and freely, slips of this and seedlings of that; but if you ask how to treat them, all he will probably say is: "Well, *I* always dibble them in somewhere shady for a start, and dust a pinch of soot round them—but maybe you will find a better way." Experience is the only schoolmaster he trusts; and in the same way as he has learnt everything for himself, so he would like to see other people trusting in nobody but themselves. The result, so far as his own garden is concerned, is admirable. Some would say he has green fingers; but Charlie himself would say it was all a matter of common sense—and faith in his own ability.

I remember a talk I had with him one day in autumn. His cottage lies well back from the road, shut away from passers-by by the whole width of his crowded garden. I heard his ladder rustling among the gay, withered leaves; he was gathering his apples. I opened the rickety gate under the ivy-tod, walked up the cobble path, and made my way round to the side of the cottage where I could just see his weathered face and shining eyes peering at me out of the apple-boughs. We talked for a while of this and that, a conversation as desultory and peaceful as the autumn afternoon itself, while the red and yellow leaves fluttered to the ground and the leviathan sunflowers, with their lesser constellations of buds, put the weakling sun above to shame. Then Charlie clambered out of the apple-tree and, setting his heaped-up basket among the windfalls that were scattered over the dark earth, came over to me in silence.

"Do you read poetry?" he asked. Assured that I did, he then added: "Maybe you write it, too?" And when the proper basis of understanding was thus secured, he put his horny fingers in his waistcoat pocket and produced a folded sheet from a small exercise-book. "Read this," he said, "and tell me what you think of it."

In a bold, straightforward handwriting three verses were written on the grimy sheet. I do not remember their entire contents, but I do remember that the first verse sang of violets ("that's Alice, when she's ten"), the second of daffodils ("that's Alice, when she's fifteen"), and the third of roses ("that's Alice, when she's twenty").

I suppose there are few minor situations more embarrassing to the conscientious than to be given some verses to read and then to be asked, by their author, for a candid criticism. Inferior verses are bound to mean more to the poet who writes them than to the reader who reads them: the former at least knows what fine emotions he intended to convey, and those emotions surround his verses like an aura which only he can wholly divine. Of course, one could behave like the Rev. Twopenny, of Little Casterton, to whom Clare sent his early poems in the hope that this worthy gentleman might help him to get them published. Mr. Twopenny merely sent the poems back again "with a cold note stating that he had no objection to assist in raising the poor man a small subscription, though the poems appeared to him to possess no merit." Clare retaliated later by lampooning the clergyman in some witty couplets that made good use of his unfortunate name; and perhaps Charlie would have revenged himself on me in the same manner, if I had adopted a similarly tactless attitude.

Instead, by as happy a route as I could discover on the spur of the moment, I led the conversation away from the particular to the general, and before either of us really knew what was happening we were engaged upon a discussion concerning the diverse nature of verse and poetry.

It was during this talk that I first discovered how far afield Charlie's interests roamed beyond the confines of his flowery garden. Milton, I happened to say, was an example of the entire poet. "Now there," Charlie replied, "I don't agree. I think *Paradise Lost* is a poor sort of poem: most of it is full of words I can't understand, anyway—and there's no *life* in it."

Somehow this brought up the subject of music. "I dare say you'll think differently," said Charlie, his diamond eyes brightening as his mind grew heated with the ideas that delighted him: "I've my own notions about music. You see those trees over there" (and he pointed towards some yellowing willows slanting over the pond beside his garden), "well, *they're* music to me. So's somebody leading a good life. Or a child picking flowers in the fields. All that's what I mean by music."

From any English hedgerow

And when the conversation, following its own inconsequent course, came back again to poetry, Charlie said: "My favourite poet is Shakespeare. There aren't many evenings go by but I read something or other out of one of his plays. I wonder if you know this bit?"—and then, not so much to impress me by the intimacy of his acquaintance with the playwright's work as to share with me his obvious delight in it, he quoted, giving each slow word a native accent that Shakespeare would surely have relished, Jaques' speech on the seven ages of man.

I suppose Charlie is somewhere about fifty years old. He has never lived anywhere but in this same cottage, which was his father's and his grandfather's before him. His father was one of the last, hereabouts, of those small cultivators whose doom was sealed with the advent of Enclosure. From him, no doubt, Charlie inherits the iron determination with which he still makes his stand against a world of big-scale farming for profit.

Exactly what he lives on nobody knows, yet he never seems to be in want. Occasionally he may get an order for a score of hurdles from some farmer who happens to be old-fashioned enough to prefer them. He sells a few vegetables and apples to his neighbours; and once or twice during the course of the year he may lend a hand to some smallholder in the district. On the proceeds of all this (and perhaps on such savings as have survived from the days before the last war, when he rented an orchard and kept a fair number of chickens) he and his sister live to-day, maybe meagrely, but certainly happily.

Indeed, Charlie is one of the most truly happy men I know. His life may be circumscribed but it is full. Change and variety from the outside world he never seeks: he does not even bother to go as far away from home as the village. Many a time I have asked him if he would not come along and see my garden—a matter of ten minutes' walk; but he just smiles and says, "I don't know, I never seem to have the time."

Though he is something of a recluse, there is nothing shy or withheld about him, once you get to know him. In conversation he is brisk and vivid, and he is in close touch with every aspect of the immediate life around him. Every dawn sees him out in his garden.

"That's the time I like best," he says; "everything is fresh then, and new. Even the air seems cleaner." (Not that it could ever be called dirty, in so open and uncontaminated a spot.) "I like to go and stand down there by the pond and see the primroses reflected in the water. And there's nobody about anywhere: only me and the birds and the animals."

If Charlie does venture beyond his garden (other than on those rare occasions when he goes away to work), it is usually at night.

"I was up by the cross-roads at Robin's Head at midnight last night," he once said, "and whose voice do you think I heard? Yours!" Now Robin's Head is at least three-quarters of a mile away from my house, as the crow flies; yet when I recollected what I had been doing at midnight, I found he was certainly right. A night of extraordinary starry brilliance had persuaded me out into the garden; and Charlie, with an ear as keen as a Red Indian's, had heard my voice if not my actual words.

Another midnight walk he told me of was to a place locally known as the Churchyard. It is a meeting of four green rides, far out in the middle of the fields, with not even a barn near by, much less a church. The place is legend-haunted. There is a pond, rush-fringed, close by and in summer the air smells sweet of thyme and marjoram.

"They've a saying round here," said Charlie, "that if you go to the Churchyard on midsummer night, and stand by that little pond at midnight, you'll hear bells chiming. The sound is supposed to come from some church bells buried in the water. Old Tom Selby will have it there was once a church there, and others will tell you the same. Some say it's where they buried those who died of the plague, donkey's years ago. But nobody seems to know the rights of it all. Anyway, I thought I might as well go and see if I could hear the bells!"

Charlie's laugh made it clear he had gone less in expectation of hearing any bells chiming in the water than because the lonely, haunted place attracted him as just right for a midnight walk. He would certainly have it all to himself.

Although there is this streak of fancifulness in Charlie's make-up, he nevertheless mostly keeps strictly to facts. Of a bundle of books I once gave him, ranging from anthologies of poetry, through Henry Williamson's *Tarka the Otter*, to Samuel Butler's *Erewhon*, it was the last that most forcibly appealed to him. The poetry books he prized in the main because they provoked his own gentle muse, whilst he relished *Tarka the Otter* for the multitude of its close, natural observations which he could check and query from his own intimate knowledge of nature. But *Erewhon*, I found, was something entirely after his own heart. Butler was a rebel, Butler said audacious things. And Charlie, who, in his own quiet way, is also a rebel, sometimes likes to suppose that he too is saying audacious things.

"I'll tell you what I've been thinking," he said one day. "Most people hold that selfishness is a bad thing, but I don't agree. When you've *earned* a thing by your own work—whether it's a flower in your garden or a thought in your mind—you *ought* to be selfish about it. That's good: what's bad is envy of things belonging to somebody else, things you haven't earned for yourself."

The value of such remarks may not be in their profundity—most of Charlie's sayings are apt to sound platitudinous until you recall the fact that they spring from his own individual thinking. They are original enough to him; and, like his verses, they are perhaps more calculated to thrill the teller than the told. I think Butler pleased Charlie because he was so eminently sane. He took nothing for granted. What tradition and the pundits agreed was final was not final for Butler until it tallied with his own conviction. And I think Charlie saw in himself another Butler, testing everything by his own experience, accepting nothing at second hand. His opinions, if faulty or even trite, are at least his own. It is imperative to bear this in mind when talking with him, and more than once I have had occasion to remember what Edmund Blunden wrote of Clare, "Tact was essential if you would patronize him: you might broaden his opinions, but you dared not assail them."

Modern education will see to it that there are very few Charlie Beslyns in the future. To achieve such contentment, in a world bounded by an acre of clay, will be difficult indeed when every country child has been perfectly moulded into the urban pattern which modern methods of education are designing for him.

Charlie digs in his garden. He pauses a while, and a robin comes and perches on his fork. He looks around him—these are his flowers, his apple-trees, his cottage. Every sound yields up its meaning to him, as he stands there listening in the still, sunny afternoon; and his eye, bright as the robin's, misses nothing of the small, eventful movements that are going on all around him. If, in such a simple scene, he is happy, it is because, by desire and by tradition, he is satisfied to suck the nectar from whatever flowers may come his way. Utterly self-reliant, and disciplined to the fewest possible needs, I think I can honestly say he comes as near as any man I know to the power of seeing "a world in a grain of sand, and a heaven in a wild flower." And for this power he has absolutely nobody but himself to thank—himself, and the enigmatic fate, perhaps, that caused him to be born of simple country stock.

To be country born and bred must count for less and less as the years go by: it counts for less already. Here, in Larkfield, in common with most other villages to-day, as soon as the children are comfortably able to make the journey, they are whisked off by 'bus to the nearest considerable town (in this case eleven miles away) where they attend an up-to-date school complete with every possible amenity that modern educational theories can devise. Since the town is so far away, the 'bus, which must needs make a circuitous journey in order to pick up the children from outlying villages, leaves Larkfield at eight o'clock in the morning. Some of the children have half an hour's walk before that, and another half an hour's walk when the 'bus deposits them on the green at five o'clock in the evening. Thus their homes become little more than dormitories to them and they have less and less opportunity to indulge that busy idling, in lane and meadow and wood, which is the basis of every country child's development, an education such as no school can possibly improve upon and a sure foundation for that after-contentment which makes Charlie Beslyn the happy man he is.

Nor is this the only, or perhaps even the worst, penalty which must be paid by these country children who are the compulsory victims of the increasing trend towards a centralized education. Spending so considerable a proportion of their time in the towns, they must inevitably adopt town habits of thought and feeling. They mix with town children, playing and working with them throughout the day. They are taught by teachers who, whatever the consequent advantages may be, are at least at a disadvantage in their enforced remoteness from those peculiar qualities that characterize the rural mind. And in their free moments they rush into the streets and dawdle about the sixpenny stores and the cinemas, and so forth.

At the moment all this is not so important as it will be presently. The age at which the children are sent away to the town schools is now from ten years to eleven; but presently, as the system gets hold, and easier methods of transport are devised, the central schools will open their maws wider and country schools will become a thing of the past.

And then where shall be found a genuinely country-minded child? Hygiene is no wise substitute, in the long run, for hours spent in the open air, nor lessons in trigonometry and biology a profitable exchange, at such an age, for an education that comes as much from sauntering round the fields with a ploughman father as from the teachers themselves.

Where the children are educated (however inadequately, from the pedantic point of view) in the countryside that is their home, at least some of them may grow up preferring the country to the town, a farm-hand's job to a mechanic's. What is more, it is just in those first fifteen years that they will realize, if ever, the love of the land that is their heritage. A good farm-hand, or even a good farmer, does not acquire his most valuable knowledge of the land in school or college; and he is severely handicapped when his contact with it is cut short in those early, precious years. We complain that men cannot be induced to stay on the land these days, even when they like the work and are so eminently adapted to it. Are they any more likely to prefer it, one wonders, when the whole of their training is framed to thwart their initial advantage and to encourage them away from it?

And so I suppose we must make up our minds to accept a future in which the villagers will all speak the same standardized speech and in which the land is farmed by men trained in town laboratories. Well, I suppose it will be a more efficient world than now—if efficiency is your aim. But for my part, when I talk with Charlie in his garden, among that fruitful and pleasing higgledy-piggledy of flowers and vegetables, I cannot help believing that efficiency is a dead thing in comparison with such purposeful individuality.

Towering over Charlie's cottage is a walnut-tree. It must be over forty years old, because he says he planted it when he was a boy. From an insignificant two-leaved stick to a multitudinously branched tree, bearing all the winds of heaven, he has watched it grow, year in, year out; and if any man can be said to know a tree, that man is Charlie and that tree his walnut-tree.

In spring, on his way across the garden to feed his hens, he will snick off one of the oily leaves and press it against his nostrils: the very breath of the young year is there, in that bruised tender bit of green. And in autumn, when the leaves begin to spin and fall, he will take a long pole and thrash down what nuts he can reach, leaving the rest to fall of their own accord, so that he may shuffle the ruck of dead leaves aside and enjoy a second crop. All seasons and all moods he knows that tree. As he sits by the fire in winter, pencilling some sentiment in homely verse, he hears the wind flailing its bare boughs; and in summer its ample shade is his cool retreat at noon.

I do not wish to give the impression that Charlie is sentimental about his tree: it is perhaps typical that, although it is among the best-loved things in his garden, he keeps his winter-wood stacked untidily against its trunk to drain, and pens his chicken under its shade in summer. But then, there is no sentimentality in Charlie's attitude to anything in nature. There is his walnut-tree, and he accepts it; and use and beauty are inextricably twined in his enjoyment of it. Forty and more years he has known it; and as it broods over his cottage now, sturdy and slow and fruitful, it might well be considered an epitome of his own life, deep-rooted in one place, rich in its strong individuality.

One day, just before this snow first fell, Charlie asked me if I would lend him a history-book. Not, he stressed, one that was little more than a string of dates with their appropriate events, but a detailed history of the reigns of Richard II and those monarchs immediately preceding him.

I was a little surprised at the request. What new adventure of the mind was he embarking on now? Then he explained.

"You see," he said, "I'm thinking of re-writing Shakespeare!"

A twinkle from those black eyes somewhat relieved my momentary embarrassment. All the same, I knew that he was not wholly joking.

"I think Shakespeare got King Richard all wrong," he continued, "and it's up to somebody to put things straight again. The dead can't speak for themselves and so I'll try to speak for them. *Have* you got a history-book like I said?"

And what, I would like to know, is one to do about a man who wants to re-write Shakespeare?—even one of the thirty-seven plays. You may reply that if Charlie, in his youth, had been whisked off by 'bus to the Central School (and thence, maybe, to the High School, and thence, again, to the University) he would have acquired a perspective that would have corrected such errors in taste.

I agree. But a Charlie Beslyn, educated through High School and College might very well have lost, for all his gains, just that one quality which is to-day his abiding solace and makes him the full man he is. Charlie is an example of the natural man, and the natural man will certainly offend the canons of the school-men.

Anyway, nobody will suffer because he is to-day sitting before the fire in his English igloo re-writing *The Tragedy of King Richard the Second*; and he himself may learn quite a lot by doing so.

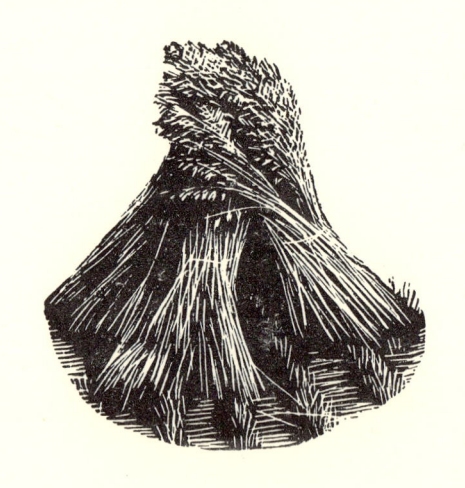

Chapter Six

WRITING verses is not the only accomplishment of which Charlie Beslyn could boast, if boasting were his pleasure. He also plays the piano. Perhaps that is too positive, too forthright a description of what actually happens when Charlie draws a chair up to his fretwork-panelled piano and picks out his favourite melodies, note by note. His own description is better: "Of course it's only a while-time," he says; "I'm no pianist."

But the merit of Charlie's piano-playing is not in proportion to its dexterity: he plays because he likes the sound of the notes, and because he likes the way they gradually fall into a recognizable sequence under his hesitant touch. And that, I contend, is merit enough. There are more proficient pianists in the village, but I honestly doubt if their enjoyment is keener than Charlie's, as his rough, unagile fingers stumble over the yellowing keys. His enjoyment in his music is the same as his enjoyment in his verses: both may be untutored, and, indeed, rather infantile, but they nevertheless spring from the pure source of all aesthetic pleasure.

I have never yet been able to persuade him to play to me. With diffident pride he will show me his verses, but apparently as yet he has less confidence in his music. All the same, without his knowing it, I have occasionally heard him play. Sometimes, of an evening, as I passed by his cottage, I have heard him trying to marshal the obstinate notes into a melody, and I have stayed a while out in the roadway, listening.

"I heard you playing the piano last night," I will say to him the next morning, when I find him digging in his garden.

"Could you make out what I was playing?" he will ask, smiling rather anxiously, like a child eager for praise which he fears he may not have earned.

"Of course," I answer; "it was 'Drink to me only.'"

"That's right," comes Charlie's happy reply; "so it was." And his simple pleasure is a joy to see.

Yes, Charlie's performances may be meagre enough, judged from an artistic point of view, but they represent something quite unique in the equipment of the average village.

Larkfield, not unnaturally and certainly not unkindly, treats them as rather a joke; but then so many things about Charlie are a joke to the villagers. How should they realize that here is a bud of culture vainly striving to break into flower? Culture is something quite outside the ken of most of them—and I am speaking particularly, of course, of farm-hands and their families. And so they smile at Charlie's efforts at piano-playing, or whistle loudly when they overhear him from the road. They go home and turn on the wireless. There's music for you! Symphony concerts and chamber-music, organ music and opera, anything you want, and all for the turning of a knob. The Wurlitzer throbs in the front room, rattling the china in the cupboard and filling the place with oceans of sound. How shall Charlie's fumbling melodies, one note now and another ten seconds later, compete with such expert performances? And yet I swear they are worth all the radio sets in the village and should be honoured for the heroic fight they put up against the victorious onslaught of Music at Second-hand.

Perhaps Larkfield is more than usually philistine in the matter of music. There are villages in Wales and in the North where it seems to be as natural for the people to sing as it is for them to speak. This certainly cannot be said of us. I have heard it ingeniously suggested that this dour songlessness may have something to do with the clay on which we live—clay that pulls the heart out of a man when he must struggle with it every day of the year. But for myself I doubt whether there is anything worth a second thought in this pretty theory. There was plenty of singing here once upon a time.

"They say times are better now," I remember one old man here saying to me, "with less work and more play. They say we worked so hard and so long that we hadn't any time left to enjoy ourselves. I dunno so much about that. Why, in them days, after ten or twelve hours' scything in the harvest fields, you'd hear men go home at night singing; and it weren't always for the beer inside 'em, either!"

And only yesterday Mrs. Trugget was telling me of the dancing and singing that used to go on over at the Pig and Whistle. "They cut the floors up no end with all their carryings-on," she said. "They used to dance to—

> I'd rather have a guinea than a five-pound note.
> For the guinea would sink and the fiver would float:
> So I'd rather have a guinea than a five-pun' note!

and all sorts of nonsense. And the bricks were all worn thin as paper with the tread of their feet."

Well, you can count yourself lucky, these days, if you hear so much as an accordion in the pubs round about here, and I never yet heard men coming out of the harvest fields singing. Evidently something has taken the song out of the people.

Every now and then, of course, the old vocal conviviality comes alive again. I remember such a resurrection of song some eight or nine weeks after the outbreak of war. We had gone into Castle Oliver in the local 'bus that shakily plies the seven miles between here and that quiet little town on market days and Saturdays. On market days the 'bus is full of farmers and their wives bent on business, but on Saturday it is full of villagers out to enjoy themselves. With money in their pockets, they crowd into the 'bus, spend the afternoon trailing round the streets and listening to the Cockney Jews touting their wares in the Square, and then visit the little local cinema in the evening.

There was a full moon that Saturday night, and Castle Oliver, as we walked through its blacked-out streets on our way to the waiting 'bus, between the gabled and overhanging houses, might have jumped back through the centuries to medieval days. There was none but pedestrians in the streets, shuffling and whispering in the moonlight, and the peaked roofs, clear-cut against the winter sky, reminded us of the drawings by Dürer. Then we all clambered into the 'bus, settled ourselves down, and began the darkened journey home.

No sooner had we got outside the little town, to where the thatched cottages stood in moonlit isolation among the fields, when somebody started to sing; and at once the whole 'busful of happy passengers joined in. With dimmed headlights we crawled through the winding lanes, while the searchlights flowered from their long stalks in the sky around us, and the singing grew to such a volume that it seemed we must be heard miles away.

Only now and then did it cease, when the lights went on and the 'bus stopped to let somebody down. "Good night, John; good night, all!"—and then, with the dousing of the lights again, the singing recommenced. And the songs we sang? Mostly they were the favourites of the minute, tunes popularized by the various radio dance bands in the frantic attempt that was being made just then to discover patriotic marching tunes for the troops. We didn't always get the melodies right and we couldn't always remember the words; but our singing nevertheless served its purpose. Some mood of unusual happiness had communicated itself to us—maybe from the full moonlight outside, or, who knows, from the novelty of a 'bus ride in the early days of the wartime black-out—and we had need to sing. And for once we responded to that need, without let or hindrance, as Mrs. Trugget's dancers did and those harvesters coming home from the fields.

Such vocal conviviality, however, is unusual. It seems we have lost the very desire to sing. And such attempts as have been made, at one time or another, to bring music into Larkfield have rarely met with much success. There was, for example, Mrs. Glow, whose whole life, one might say, was spent in a missionary endeavour to teach us the delights of good music. She played the organ at the church and gave pianoforte lessons to such as could afford her admittedly modest fees. She even composed music and once (at her own cost) achieved the dignity of print. "Ivydene: a Waltz. Composed by Ada Glow, *née* Huggins. Copies to be had of the Author." She kept a tin trunk full of copies of her waltz which she sold, at a handsome discount on the printed price, to her pupils. But they, alas, never amounted to many, with the result that when she died, worn out in an uneven struggle against the forces of darkness, the tin trunk still remained half full of clean, mint copies.

Perhaps the peak of her proselytizing endeavours was reached one day when she was asked to provide some *entr'acte* music for a play that was to be performed in the village. The play was intended (or so the performers themselves had previously advised us) to be hilariously funny; but either the acting was very bad or we were very dense, for laughs that evening were few and far between. Nor did Mrs. Glow help matters much by playing the slow movement from Beethoven's "Sonata Pathétique" between the acts. But, as she afterwards said, "One had to do what one could to raise the tone of the occasion."

That, in fact, was just where Mrs. Glow failed with us. She did not know it, and she certainly would have refused to admit it, if somebody had pointed it out to her, but her failure was largely due to the fact that she was much too intent upon improving us.

She should have taken a leaf out of the book of one of our neighbouring villages. There is still music in Toddington, and plenty of it, too. Captious residents in the place are even heard to declare that there is too much of it, especially on summer evenings, when the vicar conducts his little brass band out on the green. On those practice evenings the village heart-beat quickens, as the well-known tunes surge over the hill. There is no point in talking, then: the only thing to do is to keep quiet, or sing with the band. Down in the valley the men pause in their gardens. "There's Freddie's band at it again," they say, trying to catch the tune as it flows down to them in waves.

"Freddie" is the vicar, and he would be the very last person to object to such familiarity. He organized the village brass band, whose members are drawn solely from the workers—the blacksmith, the shepherd, old Fairy the stockman, and the lads who ride off to the jam factory each day on noisy motor-cycles—for no other reason than because he knows there is nothing so tonic as being able to make a loud noise. When inviting subscriptions from the Hall, of course, he said a band would help to hold the village together; but his honest reason for undertaking the adventure was that he knew it would be a handy means of letting off steam. He is fond of letting off steam himself. It never occurred to Freddie that, for instance, the music might improve the villagers: to act the part of cultural ambassador was never in his mind.

So the band was started and soon became a great success. There was never much finesse about its performances, and neither Freddie nor his bandsmen ever showed much desire to tackle music that wasn't chiefly noticeable for its good, broad tunes: the broader the better. In matters of expression, maybe, it ran to extremes: its "louds" were loud enough to blow the walls out, when it practised in the schoolroom, and its "softs" were a whisper to melt the heart, and the alternations between these two extremes were swift and dramatic.

However, the band achieved its purpose, and achieves it still. Like Charlie Beslyn's piano-playing, it may be no more than a "while-time," with no pretensions to professionalism and no aspirations to culture, but it is something the village does for itself and loves doing. Mrs. Glow would have considered it vulgar; but the point is that, whereas her efforts in Larkfield came to nothing, Freddie's, in Toddington, prosper with each succeeding year.

The trouble is we have no leader, nobody willing to take such matters in hand, no exuberant Freddie to push brass instruments into our hands and to gather us round him on the village green. There are men and women of talent among us, even, so the papers say, of genius: a playwright, an actor, a singer, and so on. But they are not perhaps the right persons to lead us: they are with us (if only for week-ends), but not exactly of us.

And even if they were the right persons, they have no time for us. An actor whose voice is known and admired on both sides of the Atlantic, and a playwright whose plays are certain winners—how may we reasonably expect them to spare their precious minutes for the likes of us? We are one with the trees and fields among which they come, in luxurious motor-cars, each week-end, to relax after the ardours and endurances of a week in town. We see them pass in the street, shining, fleeting presences; but we never think of them as one of ourselves—we wouldn't dare.

And so, for lack of a leader, we go songless, save for such untutored outbursts as in the 'bus that night coming home from Castle Oliver, and bandless, save for the second-hand music doled out to us over the radio; and such actor talent as there may be among us seems doomed to hide its light for ever under a bushel.

Even in the matter of book-reading we are not much better off. If the roofs were lifted from all the houses in the village to-night, at this very minute, I doubt whether half a dozen people would be discovered over a book. Mind you, I would not by any means count this necessarily to our discredit as a community. There are times when I find myself heartily in agreement, for instance, with Jack Deeping's remark to me one day when I talked with him in the rickyard up at Brock's Hole. He was cutting out some hay for fodder. Somehow the talk came round to flax, its culture and its possibilities to-day. Jack paused, his thick knuckles clenched over the handle of the hay-knife.

"I dunno," he said; "some says one thing, and some says another. I was readin' all about it in the *Farmer and Stockbreeder* the other day. But there, you could read a book as big as this here haystack about it and be no wiser—till you'd tried it out for yourself."

All the contempt and suspicion of the farmer and the farm-hand for mere book-learning was in his words. "A book as big as this here haystack!" The countryman's knowledge is gained at first hand and the subtle vagaries of nature have taught him that, until he has tried a thing out for himself and made it part of his own immediate experience, he had better not put much trust in it. No doubt this way may seem to waste a lot of valuable time. No doubt it makes him obstinately conservative. But it also makes him sure. What he knows, he usually knows beyond all contradiction, because he has proved it by his own experience. His own experience, in fact, is the touchstone by which he has learned to judge all things; and books, however wise, however time-saving, are not his experience but somebody else's. Though they be as big as "this here haystack," they count for nothing beside his own direct and personal experience.

There is much to be said for such an attitude and, of course, much to be said against it. At its worst it may make a man ignorant and sottish; but at its best it may make his character sweet and wholesome as an apple. There are old men and women in Larkfield in this year of grace, nineteen hundred and forty, who cannot even write their own names, let alone read what someone else has written; but for sheer beauty of character—sheer soundness of character— I would not know where to look for their equal. Certainly I would not look for it among the so-called wise men of this world. Statesmen are wise, but look where their wisdom has led us! Scholars are wise, but how often they miss the truth!

And that is what I mean when I say I do not altogether count this lack of book-learning to our discredit as a village community. When I talk with some of our number who *do* profess to be book-lovers, I do not feel convinced that they are thereby much superior to those who don't.

Mrs. Crosbie, who lives in one of the larger houses in the parish and occupies at least some of her considerable leisure in organizing the various activities run in connection with the church, receives a library book regularly every week, by post. She may be reckoned as one of our more knowledgeable book-readers. When I last spoke to her, she was busily engaged in getting through *Gone with the Wind*. She evidently found it hard work. "It's such a *very* long book," was the most sensible comment upon it I could evoke from her. On another occasion she declared, with perfect ingenuousness, that it was essential to read such books in order not to feel "out of things" when one was invited to dinner and a game of cards.

Of course it would be foolish to claim that Mrs. Crosbie represented the summit of village pretentions to literary culture. Nevertheless, she is far from being unique.

How much preferable, I cannot help thinking, to be like the majority here, and read no books at all!

Or, better still, to be like old Mrs. Whillum, who lives in a thatched cottage on the outskirts of the village and sits all day sewing under the eye of her sailor husband looking down at her from his black frame on the wall. At least, she used to sit sewing all day; but either her hands got clumsy from the pain of too much rheumatism in her knuckles, or the ladies in the village who used to bring her work have found that they must do without her help until the war is over; for now she has less and less to do, though the Hall still sends her curtains and chair-covers to be mended on occasion and there is usually some cottager who wants a pair of inherited trousers adjusted to his measurements.

But she always used to be so busy that somehow I never even supposed she had time for reading books. All day she sat over her sewing-table, with yards of chintz flowing away from her and swamping the little front room with billows and waves of gay colour. But the other day I found her sitting at the table with a book.

It was *Pilgrim's Progress*.

"Not that I've much need to be reading it again," she said,

"for I almost know it by heart. Now *he* went through something, didn't he?"

I picked up the coverless copy and looked at some of its extremely fanciful illustrations. She had read it she did not know how many times, she said, because she loved it and because there was nothing else to read.

"Mrs. Stowe sent me up some books a while since," she continued; "here they are." And she showed me a collection of Victorian religious books—*The Harp and the Crown*, and suchlike. "But I'm not all that much goody-goody," she laughed, turning over their pages with scorn.

"But *Pilgrim's Progress* is a religious book, too?" I said.

"Ah, but that's different. There's something so *deep* about that book—I don't know what it is. I love that book. But these—ugh! A lot of sanctimonious nonsense, that's what they are. But there's one book here I think must have got into the bundle by mistake. Here, do you know this?"

She handed me a closely printed copy, scrubby and yellow-paged, of Smollett's *Humphrey Clinker*.

"But you haven't read all through that?" I asked, turning over the pages of infinitesimal print, made even more undecipherable by the fading of the paper.

"Indeed I have," came the prompt reply. "Every word of it. And there's nothing sanctimonious about that book!"

Smollett was just a name, like any other, to Mrs. Whillum. She had never had to read him for examination purposes. She had never had to read him so as not to feel "out of things." By an accident his book had come her way and she had sensed at once that here was something real, something drawn from life itself, with all its crudities and contradictions, all its sentiment, all its lack of fair play. Not for nothing had she been a sailor's wife! Living, he had led her a pretty dance—or so I gathered from some of the remarks she occasionally let fall; and dead, his basilisk eye still stared down at her out of the frame on the wall, while she sewed all the hours there were, to eke out her old age pension. But this much at least she had gained from him, a knowledge that life is hard for most people and a detestation of all that would pretend it was otherwise.

"Mind you," she said, as she took Smollett from me and put him back on the shelf, "I won't deny the book was a bit strong in places! But there, who's the worse for a bit of strong meat now and again?"

Smollett and Bunyan: it might seem at first sight that Mrs. Whillum's two favourites have little enough in common. And yet that would not be true. They have in common the one sure touchstone of all great literature: their art is founded on the truth alone. Bunyan gives us the saints and Smollett the bawds; but both paint their pictures in hues of recognizable veracity. And Mrs. Whillum, sixty-five years away from the little village dame-school that was all her education, had at once sensed this fact. Not for her the cloud-cuckooland literature of the *Harp and the Crown*.

So while there are still Charlie Beslyns and Mrs. Whillums in our English villages, I do not think we have overmuch to fear from the taunts of those urban journalists who persist that in reality the countryside is the heart of darkness.

If they really wanted it, I could give them plenty of evidence to the contrary.

One piece of evidence springs to my mind immediately: not, it is true, from Larkfield itself, but from another village not many miles away.

I was living in a cottage next door to a gamekeeper. The gamekeeper's wife was a quiet, grey-haired woman who had lived all her life in cottages far out in the fields and woods, as gamekeepers' cottages usually are. Their quietness seemed to have entered the secret core of her. When she spoke, it was like birds twittering in a thicket. When she laughed, and that was quite often, it was like a shallow stream in the woods, burbling among the stones. She had their quietness and she also had their strength. You may have had to listen close to hear what Mrs. Dickson was saying to you; but you minded it well, when you heard it.

She was the best the countryside can breed. Towns she had never known. "I never did live within sight of somebody else's chimney-pot," she said, when her children tried to persuade her to go and live among friends in the town, "and I'm sure I don't want to begin now." And all she knew she had taught herself. She knew almost as much about the wild life of the woods as her husband; and when it was so dark outside that I could not see my hand before my face, she would find her way across the fields by trees that to me were invisible.

But what I want to tell about her concerns quite another aspect of this true gentlewoman. Her daughter Bertha cooked for me and looked after my cottage. If I was away, her mother would come round and sit in my rooms while Bertha cleaned up the place. The sun shone on my cottage in the morning and on hers in the evening; and she liked to follow the sun.

One day I missed a copy of a book of my poems, and when I mentioned it, Bertha said: "I hope you don't mind, but mother's got it indoors." I supposed the old lady had borrowed it just out of curiosity, because she happened to know the man whose name was on the title-page, and I said no more about it. But that afternoon, when Bertha had left, Mrs. Dickson came knocking at my door and handed me my book.

"Here it is," she said. "I don't want it any more, thank you, because I've copied out the only poem I like."

"And which was that?" I asked.

Apparently it was the first poem in the book that had taken her fancy, a poem of about a hundred pentametre lines; and she had copied out every word of it.

"Wait a minute and I'll show it to you," she said, hurrying away. When she returned, she handed me a large, scrubby exercise book. "There it is," she said, and pointed to my poem written inside in pencil in large, honest script.

The end of the day

I turned over the pages. There were other entries, bits of poems, odds and ends of prose, little scraps of literature that had so pleased her that she wished always to have them handy.

"And you'll never guess," she went on, "what a comfort that old book has been to me. Nights I've lain abed, when Harry was out in the woods, never knowing what had happened, never even knowing if he'd come home alive or dead, and I've comforted myself with some of the things I've written down in these pages."

Charlie Beslyn, then, and Mrs. Whillum, Freddie the vicar and old Mrs. Dickson—such, it seems to me, are the props on which our village culture rests. Not on Mrs. Glow, with her itch to improve us all, nor on Mrs. Crosbie, with her library subscription ticket bringing the latest book hot from town, nor even (nay, here least of all) on the radio, with its chamber-music and its symphony concerts poured over us all like the rain, that falls on those who want it and on those who don't, in season and out.

Culture is worth nothing, and less than nothing, if it is not made part of one's own personal experience. Not all the odds and ends of Mrs. Dickson's scrap-book (my own poem included) were worthy to be ranked under the glorious banner of literature. But she had got from them all they had to give, and no author could wish for more from his readers. For my part, I know that it was one of the proudest moments of my life when I saw my poem included in that grubby, pencilled miscellany. "You'll never guess what a comfort that old book has been to me." Who could not be humble when he takes up his pen, if he realizes that such gentle spirits as Mrs. Dickson may chance to read his words and find solace in them?

And it is the same with Charlie Beslyn's hesitant tunes on his piano and Freddie's strident marches on his brass band: homely as they are, their true source is Helicon. As for advertised culture on the grand scale, we are content to leave that to others.

·   ·   ·   ·   ·

... On the outskirts of Larkfield stands a lonely old church, shut in a knoll of elms in whose swaying tops the rooks caw loudly at evening. A mere handful of people attend the occasional services that are still held there, for the church is too remote and inaccessible for the liking of an age that must have everything at its door. Architecturally it is a simple stone edifice erected in the fifteenth century: plain enough outside, now that the vandals of intervening generations have had their way with it, and even plainer inside. One thing, however, the vandals overlooked—and that, to me at least, makes all the difference.

On the north wall is a door, never used now, and moss growing over its step. Two corbel-heads once terminated the ribbed arch that spans it like a cruck. One is missing, smashed off by some zealot to whom all art was the devil's own handmaid. The other, unaccountably, he has left. One would like to think that even he, blinded with the light of his own puritanical convictions, could yet see enough to realize that here was something that must not be touched; though the true reason for his oversight is probably much more prosaic.

However this may be, there is the corbel-head to this day, a piece of sculpture to catch the breath with its beauty. It represents a boy's head, no bigger than a man's fist, and with its nose broken away and its whole face blackened from centuries of dripping rain.

How shall I tell you what that boy looks like? His lips are full, almost to pouting; and there is a hint of arrogance in his eyes, the arrogance of an aristocratic spirit. Eclectic even in youth, he is the destined conqueror. Passion is foreshadowed in those full lips and scorn in those thick-lidded eyes—a scorn that is echoed again in the very tilt of his wide-brimmed hat set above the deep fringe of his hair.

What anonymous artist wrought him there is no knowing; but certainly in this moment of creation the man touched genius, whatever else he achieved in his lifetime. This is no stylized face such as a master-sculptor, in his London workshop, might have reproduced by the dozen for the remote country churches he was commissioned to decorate. This is Somebody—as surely as Botticelli's "Portrait of a Young Man" is Somebody. Whatever else that sculptor produced, here at least he produced a work of perfection. And it decorates the unused doorway of an almost unused country church, where the rooks wheel in the wind and the long wheatfields roll up to the neglected graves.

I have never heard this corbel-head mentioned by anybody in the village, and most, I am sure, are unaware of its existence. And I am glad this is so. It lives in its own royal right now, vulnerable only to the wind and the rain. And chance will lead the feet of all who are destined to see it and to love it—as chance led Charlie Beslyn to his music and old Mrs. Whillum to her books. To advertise it for our improving, as Mrs. Glow might have done, would be to spoil both it and us. It is there for those to find who shall.

Chapter Seven

OVER the mantelpiece in my study is a mounted set of seventeen samples of local straw-plait. Their uneven ridges shine in the lamplight, flashing back a hint of summer into the wintered room. More than any picture, they tell the story of one of our most attractive cottage industries—an industry that thrived in Larkfield and the villages round about until the turn of the century.

James I worked better than he knew, perhaps, when, crossing the Border to succeed Elizabeth on the English throne, he brought a party of Scottish plaiters with him and settled them under the protection of the Napier family of Luton. In time Luton became the focus of an industry that spread so liberally into the neighbouring corn counties that, by 1875, as many as three thousand cottagers were engaged in it in North Essex alone.

Most Larkfield farm-hands could plait or braid, and it must have been one of the most characteristic scenes of the village to see them on summer evenings sitting before their doors or ambling along the lanes plaiting with quick fingers. They were one with Shakespeare's spinsters and knitters in the sun. The material they worked with was harsh and, one would have thought, intractable; but here are my samples to prove to what nimble patterns they could subdue it. From the plain and homely Shortcake to the scintillating Brilliant, all are beautiful and individual and woven with those minute variations which, although they are the bane of a machine-minded age, are one of hand-plaits' surest assets. They were plaited for me by Maria Bond, one of the few remaining old women in the village whose fingers have not forgotten their cunning in the practice of this precious craft. Maria is well over seventy years old, and when she dies, straw-plaiting, so far as this locality is concerned, will die with her. The more zealously, then, do I treasure my set of samples.

Maria lives in one of the council cottages that cluster, like a red scar, on the edge of the village. It is not exactly the sort of setting one would wish for the last of the straw-plaiters. If anybody should have a straw thatch over her head it is surely Maria; but the old cottage where she used to live, snug as a snail in its shell, was condemned by the authorities because its air-space did not conform with the regulations and because its sanitation depended upon the cleanly habits of the owner.

And so one day Maria's few belongings were piled on to a wagon (even a tin bath can look pathetic on such an occasion, much more so Maria's cane chair and bits of home-made rug), and she and they were transported to the new home. At seventy years and more an adequate air-space and an approved sanitation are no recompense for the loss of a home in which you have been born and bred: the most Maria could do, therefore, was so to arrange her belongings that the change might be as little apparent as possible. But even the furniture looked uneasy in such a brand-new setting; and four months after the move, when I asked her how she was getting on, the best she could find to say was, "Well, I'm getting *used* to it." Which means, of course, that she never will get used to it. Progress has carried her along with its relentless current and to the end she will remain still a little dazed by what has happened.

And what has happened to Maria herself has also happened to the homely craft of which she was such an adept. "You see," she says, "I couldn't possibly do it for a living now. Nobody would buy it." Then she adds, in the same resigned tone with which she might accept the inescapable chastisements of Providence itself: "Of course, it's the machines."

Exactly what those machines are, or why they have rendered useless the lovely work in which all her life she has excelled, is not her concern: she only knows that they have left her destitute in her old age and cancelled a life's ability.

Some little compensation there has been, it is true, and she is hardly to be blamed if perhaps she rates it higher than its value really is. The estimable organizers of the local Women's Institute got hold of her and on one or two occasions made her the star-turn of their handicraft exhibitions. Suddenly to become a centre of attraction like this was something Maria had never before experienced. She was taken to the county town in a motor-car. She was talked to by all and sundry. She was asked to demonstrate her craft in front of the assembly. She was photographed and her name appeared in a leaflet. And all this to-do, I suppose, must have seemed to her a sort of sunset splendour that somewhat compensated for past neglect. The machines may have taken away her livelihood but at least they had brought her fame.

I remember how, one day when she was explaining some of her patterns to me, she looked across the table, a little astonished that plaiting was apparently not entirely a mystery to me. "I suppose," she said, "you've been reading about me in the book," as though there were only one book and she its only theme.

In a corner cupboard near the fire, among her flowery china, Maria keeps the stock-in-trade of her craft. It is simple enough: a roller and board, worn thin and shiny with use, a bundle of straws, bleached and graded ready for plaiting, and a jumble of straw-splitters which, diminutive as they are, go by the pretentious name of "engines."

A comparatively few years ago such engines might have been seen in dozens of cottages in the village: now Maria's are perhaps the only ones remaining. Made either of bone or steel, they are no bigger than the kernel of a wild hazel-nut, and they consist simply of a needle-sharp prong round which radiate a number of blades, varying from three to ten, according to the grade of the straw which is to be split. A steam-hammer, weighing goodness knows how many tons and so delicately adjusted that it can fall on a pea without crushing it, is not more admirable to me than these minute instruments which, pressed between finger and thumb, into the pipe of the straw, cut the "splints" till they fall away in a whorl of golden ribbons.

"There used to be an old man," said Maria, "who lived in a cottage up by the chapel and made these engines for a living. He made them out of the leg-bone of a bullock—leastways, I think that's what it was."

Craftsmen were the salt and savour of village life, and I could not help being glad when even so minor a member of their brave community came alive for a moment in Maria's sketchy remembrance.

"I was never taught how to do plaiting," she said one day, as I sat watching her plait the thin straws with still agile fingers; "I just picked it up from my mother and sisters. Of course, mother had to go out into the fields to work, as well: all the same, she was one of the best plaiters in the village. Her Single Sevens were lovely! But then we could all plait in our home: even father."

Maria's own speciality was a complicated pattern called Brilliant. I remember the day when, with justifiable pride, she gave me the handsome samples that now glitter among my collection. She could not recall exactly how much a "score" she was paid for this queenly pattern, but it was much more than she was paid for the homelier kinds, such as Wisp or Satin, Diamond or Whipcord or Shortcake, which only fetched sevenpence or eightpence. Low as the price was, the women could often make more money from their straw-plaiting than the men could earn out in the fields. Once a week they took their coiled plaits down to the village shop, where they were inspected, measured, paid for, and finally dispatched to Luton.

Children call them the Keys of Heaven

Well, it is all ended now. The health of such crafts lay chiefly in the fact that they were indigenous to the locality. There was the corn in the fields; and in the village there was the manifold labour dependent upon that corn. In fact, corn was the fundamental reason for the very existence of the community; and if straw-plaiting was not perhaps so essential as milling or thatching or several other of the allied crafts and trades, at least it was as indigenous, and a very real part of the fabric of life in a cornland countryside. But it seems it had to go. At least—I look up again at my seventeen precious samples, eloquent in the lamplight, and wonder what progress really amounts to, after all.

Perhaps all the crafts had to go, and we waste our time when we regret their passing? I do not know: I only know that here in Larkfield even those that survive wear a dwindling, down-at-heel look.

Sam, for instance, was once an expert blacksmith as well as a farrier. There are iron window-catches and oven door-handles still in use here to show with what cunning he could contrive the delicate scrolls and spirals that were at once their use and their beauty. Yet to-day he rarely has occasion to practise even the simplest branches of his craft. And if you do find him some job to do he scarcely bothers himself to do it.

I wanted him to make me a hinge of a special sort. That was in spring. He came up to the house, produced a foot-rule from his ample hip-pocket, tapped here and measured there, and said yes, he would make me just the very thing I wanted. It did not occur to me at the time how much more interested he was in my apple-trees, then in full bloom, than in my hinge. Weeks went by and nothing happened. I called at the forge and spent many happy half-hours chatting with him over the roaring fire. What about the hinge? Yes, I should have it next week—but wouldn't I come round the back and look at his two baby pigs, "the little dears"?

Of course the hinge did not arrive. Sam, however, did arrive:

he had forgotten the measurements. Once again the foot-rule was produced. Once again the apple-trees, which by then showed fruit, were admired. So the weeks went by, and nothing happened. But Sam, *what* about my hinge? "Yes, midear, you really shall have it next week: you really shall. But just you come and see how fat my little old pigs are getting."

The summer passed, and my apple-trees were red with fruit when finally Sam came in the gateway one day, hiding the hinge behind his vast, sagging figure, like a guilty child.

"There you are, midear! Didn't I say you should have it?"

How could one possibly be angry with such a playful, guileless old man? Instead of my wrath, Sam took away with him a bunch of my flowers. I saw him shuffling down the road, sniffing his gaudy nosegay. "Mother won't half be pleased," he called back to me. And it was only when he was too far out of sight that I discovered the hinge did not fit as I intended after all.

But perhaps it is not quite fair to consider Sam as an example of the prevalent decay of craftsmanship in our villages. Last year he achieved his old age pension, and this little sense of security, after a life of heavy work, rather went to his head. If he more or less made his own time before, he certainly makes it now. Then again, despite his unquenchable good humour at his work, he would much rather have been a farmer or perhaps a smallholder than a blacksmith. Sam's vital interest is reserved entirely for his five-acre field.

I once said to him, as he stood blowing the "bellers" of his fire with one hand and mopping his forehead with the other: "If you had your choice over again, you'd never be anything but a blacksmith, would you?"

"I never had no choice," was his prompt reply. "Father was a blacksmith, and so I reckon I had to be a blacksmith, too."

Most craftsmen, upon inquiry, reveal the fact that they learned their craft from their fathers, and this is generally considered to be one of the reasons for the fine mastery they exhibit. The job comes as second nature to them: it is a knowledge in the blood as much as in the brain. Sam is no exception. A better farrier is not to be found for miles around; and, as I say, there are still plenty of extant examples of his admirable ironwork in the village. He has done his job to the top of his ability, because it was the job to which (as he considered) he was irrevocably called; but his heart is in the land.

And so, as work in the forge slacks off, and yearly there are fewer horses to be shod, he more and more gives himself over to a belated indulgence in the forbidden delights of farming. The village, it is true, is apt to laugh at his agricultural efforts. But Sam does not mind. And certainly there is nobody else in Larkfield who could wring more pleasure out of a skimpy five acres.

There is a child in Sam that all his bulk and years cannot hide, and I confess he rather toys with his field than farms it. Year after year, he has the greatest difficulty in getting it harvested. It is too much for him to do himself (though he used to mow it alone, often enough, working both by sun and moon) and casual labour is increasingly hard to find. Yet when, last year, Farmer Moore offered to plough, reap, and carry for him, if he would grant him permission to take his wagons through Sam's field on a short cut to some land of his own, Sam said no. That denial was a typical mixture of obstinacy and heroism. With Moore's wagons coming and going across his field, he would not feel that it was his and only his. All he actually said was: "They'd always be leaving my gate open, and I couldn't have that, now could I?"

At all costs, he feels, he must keep his field inviolate. It is the tangible symbol of a way of life that has been denied to him. It is his plot of dreams.

He can overlook it from the hatchway of his forge, and his eye is quite as vigilant over the barley waiting to be mown as over the horses waiting to be shod. Rain falls after a drought that had checked the crop. "That do look better by five bob a quarter a'ready," he says, appraising the freshened field from his hatch.

And when harvest comes at last, Sam just shuts up his forge altogether. If there are horses to be shod then, I don't know what happens to them: certainly no horsemen would be so foolish as to try to entice Sam away from his barley at such a time. The smile and the thunderous laugh disappear, and creases of anxiety take their place. Mrs. Merriman goes down the road at intervals during the day bearing trays (neatly covered with white napkins, for everything about Mrs. Merriman is neat and tidy) of food and drink; and Sam sits down behind his last year's stack, the gleaming scythe at his side, all his body sagging into the ground, to recover his spent strength.

Only when the last load is carried, does that endearing smile return. Once again Sam's mighty laugh is heard in Goose End, and once again he leans over his hatchway—there are two stacks to look at now—and dreams of what he will grow in his field next year. Perhaps he will plant it with trefolium—or "trepolium," as he calls it. Perhaps he will let it lie fallow. Perhaps . . . well, we shall see.

Yes, I agree it is not altogether fair to take Sam as an example of the decay of village crafts. Yet the decay is undeniable enough. Farming, like most else these days, is largely a matter of the smallest outlay and the quickest returns. The farmer knows well enough what he wants and it is part of his tradition to want only the best —the best thatching for his barns, the best gates for his fields, and so on. But the banks are pressing, and he can afford the best no longer, until at last he almost arrives at the stage of having persuaded himself that (for instance) the factory-made gates which he is compelled to set up in his fields are quite as good as any the local carpenter could make. At any rate, they are much cheaper and (so he is forced to argue) at least they will last out his time.

Thus consoled, he gets on with his job of forcing the land, instead of serving it. Never mind about layering the hedges in the good old-fashioned way: hack them down and stuff the gaps with brambles. Never mind about trimming the cornricks and decorating them with straw-cockerels: there is no time for such nonsense now. Never mind about resting the land after it has borne its best: a few sacks of artificial manure will serve just as well as a year's fallow and save a crop into the bargain.

So it goes on. To-day is all the farmer can afford to think about, who should really be thinking for his sons and his sons' sons after them. And in this general scramble to make ends meet, the craftsmen who served the farmer have been left behind. Their work may last longer, but it costs too much. It may be best suited to the peculiar needs of the locality, but it takes too long. And so, from being almost the most valuable men in the community, the craftsmen sink to the level of odd jobbers—men of a first-class ability for whom there is no longer any use.

Such a man is Josh Mengies, the carpenter. A few farmers in the parish still call on him to do little jobs for them. "I've worked on and off for him ever since I was a boy," he said of one local farmer; "he won't have strangers about the place." But for the most part he just potters about, doing nothing in particular.

Like his father before him, Josh is an excellent craftsman. His scorn for anything botched or shoddy is as strong as ever it was. I have seen a photograph of the shop in which he worked with his stern old father: the timber neatly piled for seasoning, the square-set stacks of planks, and the well-kept tools ranged above the benches. And the contrast with his own workshop to-day is less a criticism of Josh than of the way things have changed these last twenty-five years or so. One end of a double cottage serves him for workshop, and the rooms are so littered with junk that only by twisting this way and bending that can one progress from one room to another. Broken chairs, bits of window-frames, rusty iron, split sacks of cement and odds and ends of timber lie about in such confusion that even Josh himself can scarcely ever find what he is looking for.

Only the tools are still kept in order; and, although so many of them seldom get used to-day, Josh will not let anybody touch them but himself. He knows them like friends, their faults and their merits, and he cannot bear that they should be used by hands unfamiliar with their peculiar moods.

Then again, Josh is an inveterate collector of everything he can lay his hands on. Nothing must be thrown away because one day or other it may come in useful. The fact that it never does come in useful is beside the point, as is also the fact that he will soon be past using it anyway. He pulls down condemned houses and fills his yard with doors and windows and beams, and his workshop (where he can still find a corner for them) with locks and grates and oven-doors, all because he is convinced that one day they will come in useful.

One such oddment, I must confess, did come in useful—though I would perhaps have prevented it if I could. There is a small pond at the bottom of my garden which, if it is not exactly ornamental, at least serves to supply the garden with water in times of drought. The trouble is it shelves so steeply that every dip of the bucket is likely to send one plunging headlong in. So I asked Josh to come along one day and look at it. Couldn't he make me a landing-stage of some sort, so that I could stand a little way out over the water and dip my bucket without fear of falling in?

Josh paid me several visits and considered the matter very carefully. I explained how I thought the job might be done: a wooden girder here and a support against a tree there and so on. I should have known, of course, that Josh would never agree. He did not say so, outright, but I could see that he was not at all convinced. Suicide by drowning is rather a common occurrence in these parts and perhaps he wanted to be quite sure that I too did not come by a watery end. Anyway, he said he would look around: if I waited a little while he would be certain to find the very thing.

Then I went away for a holiday. When I came home the job was finished. Josh had indeed found the very thing. There is no danger now that I shall fall in when I dip my bucket, or that the landing-stage will give way under my weight. So long as iron endures I shall be safe, and those who come after me. Josh has laid the boards of the platform (themselves thick as railway-sleepers) on the discarded chassis of a motor-lorry.

"I knew it would come in useful for something," he said, proudly waiting for me to express my approval; "and there you are."

Two things you notice about Josh when you first meet him: the crystalline blue of his eyes and the lithe muscularity of his hands. Most craftsmen's hands are lean and well-shaped, trained in responsiveness, alive in every nerve; but I think Josh's hands are exceptionally fine. The whole craftsman lives in them. Age has done little to diminish either their strength or their sureness of purpose; but now they are mostly idle, their rare adaptability wasted on trivial ends.

As for his clear blue eyes, pale as ice, I sometimes wonder if they do not betoken in their unwitting owner the possession of something akin to occult sight. Perhaps I am being rather too fanciful here, but certainly Josh is proud of his prowess as a wart-charmer.

"Putting them away" is the expression he uses for this peculiar ability. I admit I have never verified his claims at first hand; but he says he has cured hundreds of warts in his time and is still ready to cure them on anybody who asks his help. He has no need even to see the person who wishes to be cured: it is apparently enough if Josh is informed of the number of warts.

Exactly what method he employs I have never been able to find out. I believe some charmers smear the warts with the slime of a snail and afterwards stick the snail on a thorn, whilst others rub them with a piece of old meat which they afterwards bury. Then there is what is known as "buying" warts. But Josh evidently favours quite other methods than these. Not only has he no need to see the warts but he also makes it a rule never to accept payment for his services. He did once own to me that he might perhaps use a certain formula of words; but on another occasion all he would admit was that "maybe I sometimes *think* about 'em, while I'm sittin' down, resting." Also, he insists that although he can "put them away" at any time, spring and summer, when the air is dry, are best.

Then, too, Josh has a more than usually happy knack in dealing with all sorts of plants and trees and animals. His fruit-trees, every one of which he has either planted or grafted himself, are some of the most bounteous in the parish; and trailing over a tumbledown shed at the back of his cottage is a grape-vine which, in defiance of all the accepted laws of nature, confronts the prevailing easterly winds with clusters of small black grapes, good for wine-making if not for eating.

Nothing appears to please him better than to be asked for advice in the matter of some fruit-trees one has planted in one's garden. It has become part of the ritual of the year that he shall come in and prune my trees for me; and I know he is convinced that, unless he does this, they will certainly not yield their best. He has told me the ancestry of most of the older trees (where they came from or who planted them) and if his names for them do not always correspond to the catalogues of nurserymen at least they are given promptly and with an authority I for one would not deny.

Like Sam, Josh rents a piece of land, though he has never bothered to plough and sow it. Instead, he allowed it to revert to grass and then he bought a colt and turned her loose in it.

It was Jessie the colt that first revealed Josh's tenderer side to me. He said there was Arab blood in her. Be that as it may, she was certainly a frisky creature. All day long she would stand about the meadow, nibbling at grass which she had long ago shorn of all its juicier blades. Then she would suddenly lift her delicate head, blow out her nostrils and neigh, and fly round the meadow in circles, kicking up a shower of turf with her slim, unshod hooves.

Mostly she was left alone all day, while Josh was out on some trivial job or other; and in her loneliness, she was glad of any attention. Children called to her as they came home from school, and passers-by stopped to stroke her and give her apples and lumps of sugar. If Jessie was glad enough of these attentions, Josh was torn between jealousy and pleasure: he liked to see her taken notice of, but at the same time he disliked to see any division of her allegiance. I don't think he need have worried. Jessie never neighed so loudly as when he arrived in the meadow every evening, bringing her hay which he stuck into the fence, or a bucket of well-water which she would empty without stopping, as if she were a suction-pump. And to attempt to entice her away, once he was anywhere within sight or sound, was a sheer waste of time.

Jessie endured all weathers and grew more tousled and more clogged with mud as the months went by. At last Josh decided she must be broken in. Night after night he encouraged her round and round, at the end of a length of stout rope. Her eyeballs shone, her young nostrils quivered. It was a game, the climax of every day's long waiting; and she never guessed that the end of it would be imprisonment between the shafts.

Josh had said he would never part with her, and I believed him. "Them old gippoes keep on botherin' me," he said. "They tell me I've only got to name my price; but I'm not selling her."

One day, however, he did sell her. What price tempted him away from his decision I do not know: or did some unvoiced necessity compel him? Jessie went. And no sooner had she gone, of course, than Josh repented of his bargain. No happy neighing greeted him now when he went up to the meadow in the evening. No use sticking armfuls of hay in the fence for her to pull at when she had finished her joyous canter. But regrets would not bring her back again; and if ever Josh thinks of replacing her, it will not be until after the war that he can do so now. Only a little while before the snow came, I saw him ambling round his meadow, nothing to do, nobody to talk to; and the peewits flying over with their melancholy wailing seemed the very voice of his loneliness.

Chapter Eight

IT may not warm the blood much, these bitter days, but at least it warms the mind, to turn over the pages of one's diary and read what one was doing in summer days gone by. What one was thinking and feeling is quite another matter and for quite another occasion. To read that I found a death's head moth in the lane on a certain July evening is far more interesting to me just now than to read of the psychological or emotional state I happened to be in at the time. Give me a bald and accurate diary of facts to read over and I am satisfied. The rest can look after itself. I was sad once and no doubt I shall be sad many times yet; but I may never again see a death's head moth in the lane by Penny Fields.

Not that only the more startling entries in such an objective diary are worth poring over. I have only to read such a simple record, for instance, as that which tells how, on March 6th last year, I saw five brimstone butterflies and a palm-willow full of honey-bees, oxlips in bud and coltsfoot in the fields by Bassetts Farm, for my mind to glow with the memory of a certain walk taken in the first flush of spring.

Such a memory almost gives the lie to present frost and snow. Almost, I say; for nothing will really gainsay this omniscient cold. Plants keep warm under snow; and even houses, it seems to me, should be warmer than they are just now for the generous white blanket with which the skies have covered them. But apparently there are no blankets that can keep out this cold. It penetrates to the very marrow. You sit over the fire (or even close inside the fire, if, as in my own case, you have an old open fireplace), and an illusion of warmth on your face at last breeds some sort of cheer in you; but your back tells the truth, and you have only to concentrate on that for a moment for the good cheer to vanish like a dream. I run my hand down the walls and discover that this north-east wind doesn't even need a cranny to enter in: defiant of mere matter, it penetrates and permeates all.

It is one of the minor irritations of a timbered room, that even in the depth of winter, when fire and lamp have made the air hot enough, bees and butterflies will tumble out of the crevices in the beams under the mistaken notion that spring has come and it is time for them to wake up. Dazed for awhile, they bask in the warmth, wash their wings free of clogging sleep, and then begin a frenzied dance of death round the lamp.

But this weather even the bees and butterflies hibernating in my beams have felt no premature urge to awaken. Pile the logs on as you will, they remain mercifully immune from any such temptation. Either that, or they are simply dead. And when I wake in the morning, to a house of unheated rooms, and see the breath rise from my mouth like steam from a singing kettle, and come downstairs to a fireplace full of dead ashes, and every blessed drop of water frozen to a block of ice—why, then I could very nearly agree that, in either case, the bees and the butterflies are better off than I!

But come, let me turn over the pages of my diary. They may perhaps help me to believe that once there were flowers in the garden and whistling thrushes in the trees and no news of wars in the papers. Call it escapist, if you like: I do not mind. Just now I would give my kingdom to escape from this annihilating cold (though of course in days to come I shall even be glad to recall it, if only as something endured and duly rewarded) and if the thought of bygone springs and summers can help me, then help me they certainly shall.

What, for instance, is this first entry for June of last year? "Went to the Essex Agricultural Show, at Braintree."

Goodness, yes, what a day of sunshine and brass bands and farmers in knee-breeches and white tents flapping in the breeze! As I sit here remembering, that day slowly comes alive for me, like a flower opening, petal by petal, in the sun.

It all began, I remember, down on the village green in the morning, where a small knot of us stood talking, while we waited for the 'bus. What the talk was all about I have now no idea; but my diary records how there were swallows "flossing" on the water, while we stood there, the sunshine lighting up the rich dark blue on their backs, as they dipped to meet their shadows and at each brief impact sent up a miniature fountain of glittering spray.

Then the 'bus arrived and off we went, stopping all along the road to pick up yet more passengers, till we could hold no more. For me, country 'buses are one of the very best contributions progress has made towards the amenities of country life, and rarely are they so attractive as on market days, when farmers and their wives, who used to spank along the road to market in their gigs, jostle and shout to one another till the conversation becomes a sort of distilled essence of all country talk. And the day we rode in to visit the Show was no exception. Small farmer, foreman, horseman, stockman—all were on holiday, shinily washed, and turned out by their wives much as they themselves, years ago, might have turned out their horses, combed and braided and cleaned to the last hair.

As for the Show itself, what I recall most vividly was watching certain events in the arena. The sun blazed and the music came in noisy gusts that made no sense so far away but were the only conceivable accompaniment to such a chatter and such a blue sky. A team of fine Suffolk horses entered close by the Grand Stand and began their slow progress round the course. Proud as the day itself, they walked in a string, announcing themselves with a chime of bells and a shifting gleam of brasses. Under their glossy chestnut skin the muscles rippled as they strained, gently and evenly, at the wagon behind them. With every lift of the foot, their long, combed fetlocks flounced like the skirts of a ballet dancer. Indeed, their whole progress round the course was like a slow pavan. By their sides trode three horsemen, trim in fawn coat and breeches, as full of pride in their charges (one of whom, I recollect, was called Stormer, and another Nelson) as we of pleasure at the sight of them. Little waves of cheering followed them round the arena till at last they drew into rank with the other entries before the judges.

Perhaps those thunderous Suffolk horses, plumed and braided, with golden moons dangling from their martingales, and sacks of corn piled so squarely in the varnished wagon behind them, have little enough to do with farming as it is practised to-day; but I know how glad I was to see them, even on a showground, and to know that there are still farmers willing to stock their farms with such noble creatures, and still farm-hands able to turn them out in this brave, traditional manner.

To see what farming actually is like to-day, and will be to-morrow, it was only necessary to walk across the field to the stand-holders' section, where every conceivable mechanical farm implement was being exhibited and explained by brisk and persuasive salesmen. Mostly, I noticed, it was the younger farmer, and farmers' sons, who showed the keenest interest here. Such older farmers as there were hovering around this shining, inhuman concourse, seemed to me to wear a sceptical mien as if to say no good could come of such devilish contrivances.

In fact, one of my plainest recollections of that afternoon is of a little group who came and sat next to me in the tea-tent. It consisted of an old white-whiskered farmer, frank and ruddy, and his two alert, well-built sons. Over the buns and the tea, thick and black as tar, the young men tried every way they knew to persuade their father to invest in a certain sugar-beet lifter that had taken their fancy among the exhibits outside. They ran over its points, but the old man looked as if he would rather they were discussing the points of a Punch or a Percheron. They demonstrated how in the end it would save time and money—but their father shook his head and seemed to imply that good husbandry was reckoned by other standards. And finally, in rising exasperation, they accused him banteringly of an obstinacy that would soon land them all in the bankruptcy court. "It's no use, Father," one of them said "if you don't mechanize, you'll go under."

I don't know whether these eager young men won their case; but in any event I don't think their old father would be convinced, however much the farm's turnover might improve.

So much for the Agricultural Show. Now what is this entry at the beginning of October? "Crab apples and sloes for jelly, gin and wine." Well, the jelly is all eaten and the wine all drunk, but something of their savour lives on in these few words recalling the dates they were gathered and made. Something, also, of the kindly atmosphere of those days—warm sunshine on newly ploughed fields, red leaves, and wasps in the fallen fruit.

Sloes are so plentiful here that it is only necessary to walk across the field at the back of my house to gather all I could possibly require. But crabs, although these also are fairly plentiful, are an adventure in themselves. Six trees in the middle of a balk that runs across a forty-acre field yielded me the fruit for my jelly that year; and clear as yesterday I remember the journey we made to fetch them in.

A flare of autumn colour ran along the hedges—maple and spindle and dogwood. Rooks and clouds were being blown pell-mell across the sky. And from a rickyard far away came the drone of a threshing-machine, the only sound in that mellow afternoon. The stubble had all been ploughed in, and the gleaming waves of the furrows still lay just as the share had turned them, shining with moisture, waiting till the wind and the frost should crumble them into a kindly tilth.

As we trudged over the heavy ploughlands to the crab-apple trees on the horizon, our boots gathered the clay in such quantities that their weight seemed like a magnet drawing us from the earth's centre. We were, as they say hereabouts, "all barmed up," but the fallen apples, speckling the clay with their blood-warm red, were a more than sufficient reward for our endeavour.

We had filled our baskets from the windfalls among the furrows, when somebody discovered that the best were in the ditch by the balk. And what I recall most of that afternoon's rich harvesting is the crunch of apples under my feet in the bottom of the ditch and the strong smell of water-mint as I picked them out. Who shall analyse why one detail of such an adventure is destined to stand out stronger than any other? At any rate, every time we opened the crab-apple jelly that year, I seemed to smell again the crushed mint under my feet; and now, when the jelly is all eaten, like a fume drifting across the mind that smell still remains.

Another entry in the diary, a week later, brings back that rich autumn mood even more vividly. "Medlars from 'Swallows,'" runs the record under October 18th: "apples and pears, bullaces and blackberries in quantities."

"Swallows" was once an outlying farm-house, though not even the foundations remain to prove its existence to-day. What does still remain, however, is a ruined close full of ancient, gnarled fruit-trees. How many years have passed since anybody pruned and tended them I do not know; but once now and then, in a year of plenty, they bear and litter the grass underneath with their unwanted fruit. Chiefly it is the medlars that draw me to "Swallows" about this time of the year; and if the jelly from them is somewhat harsh and certainly not to everybody's taste, well, there is a snobbery in jam-making as in everything else, and it is not everybody who can put medlar jelly on his table!

This particular season, however, every tree in "Swallows" close seemed to have surpassed itself. Pruning or no pruning, those old trees bore with a prodigality many a walled garden might have envied. The place was the very epitome of autumn's mellow fruitfulness. Bullaces, like peeled li-chee nuts, lay heaped in the grass. Fallen pears were so plentiful that wasp and bird had only bothered to take a brief nip out of one before passing on to another. Chestnuts had fallen, and, in falling, split and tumbled out "conkers" of a smoothness and redness and bigness that would have made any boy whoop with delight. There were plenty of medlars, rough-skinned and still as hard as stones. And trailing round the rim of the pond were bramble-bushes, heavy with their dark sprays of berries.

"Swallows" smelt of fermenting fruit, the whole of Keats' Ode concentrated in half an acre of neglected ground.

We gathered all we could carry and should have been satisfied. Instead, next day we returned for more. Perhaps it was foolish of us to expect to recapture the spirit of such a scene. Perhaps it was just one of life's little jokes—or a pertinent reminder that man cannot live by poetry alone. We pushed open the broken gate, eager to plunder the fruit a second time and to smell the winy air. A score of pigs stared at us, who had so unexpectedly interrupted them in their juicy meal. Still as stone, they glittered at us out of mean, beady eyes; and then, convinced that we were not worth their attention any further, suddenly began rootling among the fallen apples again. The final comment, I remember, seemed to me implied in the grunt of sensual satisfaction with which one of the biggest and nearest sows rubbed her scurfy buttocks up and down the bark of a tree.

Turning back the pages a month or two, I read: "July 14th. Clover cut and carted in Gilbert's Field," and a picture immediately presents itself of a high-piled wagon, its lower part just hidden beneath the dip of the hill, drifting across the horizon like a punt, with Jerry Gardiner guiding it, using his fork for a pole. I hear him calling to his brother, who leads a horse I cannot see, and sight and sound are one with the summery scent of clover drying in the sun.

But perhaps the entry of those summer months that stirs the most vivid remembrance in me is the one that reads: "August 9th.

Bankes' wheat, that has stood in traves ever since his son fell ill, is being carried at last."

Harvest is literally the crown of the year for us who live in the cornland belt: all the months lead up to it and upon its success or failure depends all we know of prosperity. No sooner is the stubble ploughed in, than the drill advances over the field, scattering the new seed, first the winter wheats, whose frail green straws now lie buried under the snow, and then the spring wheats and the barley. To casual eyes it all looks much the same throughout the spring and early summer; but as it ripens, the differences become obvious enough. Barley in ear is like fur, like a soft pelt, and it ripples like water as the wind blows over it. Gradually, as harvest-time draws nearer, the ails begin to bend over, till at last they point back to the earth instead of up at the sun. But to the very end, the wheat-heads remain erect, masculine and proud. Both fall at last, however, beneath the binder whose clatter is the best counterpart we have to-day to the sibilant scythe.

Perhaps that silvery whisper of the scythe was a fitter token of the heat and climax of the year, but the rackety-clack of the binder also has its appeal. Ears that were not trained on chamber-music find jazz the more appealing. Anyway, when the binders begin gyrating round the fields, scattering an untidy trail of sheaves with their fluttering, mechanical fingers, Larkfield touches the peak of its year's endeavour. Everybody then talks of corn. Everybody watches the weather. And everybody, from the farmer and the farm-hand himself to the visitor and week-ender, shares something of an excitement that has its origin away back in the days of the Open Field village, and even earlier, when the quantity and quality of the harvest was a measure not only of prosperity, but of existence itself.

The year of which my entry tells was the year of a bumper harvest. While plants in the gardens withered in a clay that was as hard as iron, the corn, loving such drought, flourished under the continual sun. "White unto harvest" was exactly the right

The village carpenter's handiwork

expression for those wide acres of barley and oats, whilst the wheat, burnished like copper, flashed the heat back at the sky.

All day long a series of minute explosions, like toy artillery, sounded in the wheatfields, and the farmers walked round the headlands, snatching an ear of corn and rubbing the husk away, to test the white starchy kernel between their teeth.

Of all the farms in the parish I do not think there could have been one more eagerly keyed up to the excitement of harvest than was Moat Farm, where young Bankes was taking over the management of the farm from his father. It was to be his first harvest; and with all the vigour of his twenty-one years, he prepared to greet the occasion. His binder was the first I heard in the fields in the morning and the last at night. The waking hours were not long enough to crowd in all the work he wanted to do. The sunny weather crowned his efforts, and I doubt if there was a happier young farmer in the county.

And then suddenly he collapsed and had to be carried off the field to his bed. Sickness had grabbed at him out of the skies and in a week he was dead.

Everywhere else the brisk work of harvest went on as usual: only at Moat Farm the stooks stood waiting in the fields, while their shadows wheeled around them through the empty day. The young man was buried and that afternoon the wagons came out into the field again and the interrupted harvest continued. In his black alpaca jacket Mr. Bankes loaded the sheaves: though the bottom had fallen out of his world, harvest must go on. Not a word passed between him and the farm-hand who forked up the sheaves, and the clink of the harness and the rumble of the wagon wheels only served to emphasize the silence which here replaced the laughter and banter immemorially attendant on such a task.

Slowly the loaded wagon was led into the rickyard, the black-coated farmer perched on top, like a mourning band on summer's golden sleeve.

Coppery wheat-heads in the sunshine, loaded wagons

bumping over the stubble, heat, deep drinks out of bottles cooled under the hedges—yes, my diary of brief, factual entries certainly has its gift to make. To me, anyway. Sitting here in my study, turning over its pages, I had forgotten the deep snow outside and the chilly bedroom waiting for me upstairs. For an hour I have been back again in summer.

And, believe it or believe it not, where the heat of the lamp has warmed the beams, a hidden bee is buzzing, intermittently, half-heartedly, as if even he had partaken of my illusion and were wondering whether it was time to come out of his hiding-place to greet the sun.

Stay where you are, poor misguided creature! See, I turn down the light and prepare to face the arctic regions awaiting me upstairs, and soon it will be just as cold down here. So stay where you are. Go to sleep again and enjoy the merciful oblivion nature has so unfairly bequeathed to you and not to me. It is a long while yet to summer.

Chapter Nine

FARMER DEEPING has been taken to hospital. How the old man was carried from his farm out to the road I cannot imagine, for Brock's Hole is approachable only by half a mile of unmade road which, at the best of times, is no more than a churned-up ride between overgrown hedges and, just now, is an impenetrable and continuous drift of snow. But the Deepings, widowed father, son and daughter, are used to surmounting such difficulties. There are weeks on end when they cannot get their stock to market or carry grain to the mill, and even in the height of summer no tradesman will take his goods up that tangled lane.

So I suppose they carried the old man across the fields, out to the ambulance waiting in the road. And now he lies in hospital, who never was away from his farm so many days together, and whose illnesses, through all the long years of his strenuous life, have never before earned the attention of a doctor.

Farmer Deeping, so the report went round, was breaking up at last; but when we asked Priscilla Deeping how her father was, after her first visit to the hospital, she answered: "He says it's the best holiday he ever had!" The nurses, apparently, were delighted with him and could not do enough for him, so that when last Tuesday he shyly announced the fact that it was his eightieth birthday, "they made such a fuss of him [as Priscilla said] that it has quite gone to his head."

And I'm sure I don't wonder that he should be so popular, for he is one of those increasingly rare old countrymen whose characters are as sweet as a nut and as full of goodness. Honest, cheery, and old-fashioned, preferring always the generous comment to the critical, he is gentle in all he says and gentle in all he does.

There are few things I find more calculated to restore a wavering faith in human nature than a visit to Brock's Hole, the little isolated farmstead where he was born and bred and from whose familiar shelter he was carried away on a stretcher across the snowy fields.

Brock's Hole is a farm of about forty acres—a couple of meadows and the rest all good clay arable. Its very isolation compels it to be more or less self-supporting; but if Brock's Hole were on the main road, I think it would still be run on the same principle, so long as Farmer Deeping owned it. For he is a small cultivator of the old school, one of those farmers who are gradually being squeezed out of existence and yet who are indubitably the finest type of farmer this country produces. They truly may be said to serve the land. They know every inch of their farms, they waste nothing, and they abhor all that savours of the penny-in-the-slot methods by which the modern large-scale farmer, regardless alike of the past and of the future, forces his land to give the greatest possible yield in the smallest possible time. Yet such small cultivators, masters of a husbandry that has the sanction of hundreds of years behind it, will soon cease to exist in this country—unless the debacle into which the present-day system has thrown farming does not compel a complete revision of method.

Brock's Hole lies about a mile across the fields behind my house, and a walk there in April is a progress through tethered clouds of blackthorn. Over the fields where the young wheat is sprouting, larks sing against the clear blue sky, whose clouds all seem to have come to earth and are lodged in Farmer Deeping's hedges. The farm itself, sheltered by a few elms, stands islanded in the fields, a small orchard close by, whose last year's crop still sweetens in the

Coming home from the fields

farm-house's only attic, a rickyard, where the remnants of harvest still await the dealer, a pond, and an old timbered barn.

Deeping's son, Jack, has just brought the horses in from the fields; and while he goes into the stable, the harness trailing and clanking round his feet, Prince and Lady find their leisurely way to the pond. The moorhens fly before their heavy tread, with heads thrust away out before them, urgent with the red light of their beaks, like danger-signals. Fetlock deep in the cloudy water, Prince and Lady slowly drink their fill, then lift their drooling heads and stare contentedly around them. The day's work is done, and this playful drink at the pond, often as much out of habit as out of necessity, signals their release. Not until Jack calls from the stable door do they splash their way out of the water, clumsily, thunderously, and go leisurely home. . . . It is an evening ritual that has gone on for generations at Brock's Hole, other Princes and other Ladies splashing among the water and taking their slow, dripping way back to the stable at last.

Go inside and talk with Jack and you will find in him the ideal blend of the old and the new, the ancient way and the modern. Much of his day is spent with the tractor, the economical advantages of which he is well aware, but his affection is for his horses. To bed them down after their day's work in the fields is quite as much the completion of his day as of theirs; and admirable as he is in handling the tractor, I for one prefer to see him sitting up behind Lady on one of his frequent visits to the mill.

"A tractor's essential on a farm, even of this size," he says. "You can't get on without one. All the same, I wouldn't stay on a farm a fortnight where there wasn't a horse or two as well."

The fume of petrol and the warm breath of horses—somehow he reconciles the two: accepting innovation, he yet keeps his firm hold on tradition, a young farmer in whom the best of both worlds uncommonly unite. Gently his father chides him, remembering the day when his own father's two pedigree Punches were the pride of the parish. "Our Jack," he says; "well, he isn't as fond of horses as he should be." But Jack only smiles: persuasively, he knows the way to counteract his old father's innate conservatism, safe in the self-assurance of his own sense of balance. The past was good and must be listened to; but, after all, he lives in the present.

Jack's fondness for his horses was an old story for me long before I learned just how deep that fondness went. It was the evening when his father had said, "Our Jack; well, he isn't as fond of horses as he should be." We were standing in the barn, whose dim interior was stabbed with a golden shaft of sunlight coming through the high, open door. Jack winked at me from behind his father's back, as much as to say, "There goes Father again. The same old tale—but you know what these old men are like!" And when I had said good night to Farmer Deeping, and Jack and I were walking across the yard together, "I don't know about not liking horses as much as I *ought* to," he said, "but just come over to the stable a minute; there's something I'd like to show you."

Prince and Lady were in their stalls, chumbling and chewing in the warm aromatic dusk. Countrymen are notoriously brief of speech; and when they have "something to show you," they invariably like to keep you in a mystified silence and suspense while they prepare their surprise. Jack disappeared into the darkest corner of the stable and then, after a lot of fumbling among what sounded like a jumble of harness, came back to me in the doorway with his arms and hands loaded with gleaming brasses. There were swingers and bells, rosettes and elaborately studded hame-reins, and as handsome a martingale as I have ever seen. They flashed in the last red rays of the sun, zodiacal emblems such as were the pride and joy of horsemen and carters in the days when a man did not yet count it loss of time to rise in the dark of morning so that he might polish his horse-brasses ready for a journey to market.

"There!" said Jack, "I don't suppose you ever guessed there was anybody round about these parts who still had a complete set of brasses in his stable, did you? There's everything here; and it all belonged to Grandfather. Pretty, isn't it?"

And he held the swinger up before him, like a priest holding up the monstrance, and as the dying sun flashed back from its clear brass mirror, suspended in the shining ring, he flicked the tiny bells at the side with his finger-nail till they rang sweetly, briefly, like the bells of the ministrant. Indeed, in that moment there was something priestly in Jack's simple gesture: he was commemorating a race of countrymen whose like we may never see again.

"Sometimes," he said, "I wish I could take Lady out in the road, she looks so fine rigged up in her harness."

I had supposed they were no more than relics, kept in the stable for sentiment's sake; but now I discovered that Jack sometimes dressed Lady up in all her finery and paraded her up and down the green ride in front of the house. "Of course I only do it to amuse myself," he said, shy at the confession that had escaped him and perhaps afraid that I might think it daft of him; "but I can tell you she does look pretty, braided and plumed and all."

It was beginning to get dark, or I believe Jack would then and there have dressed up Lady and exhibited her for my benefit. The mood was on him and I had happily won his confidence. . . . And now it is too late. Lady was shot yesterday; and Prince, I remember Jack telling me, is not very amenable to such nonsense.

To find a young man, these days, able to plait and braid horses and the proud possessor of a complete set of bells and brasses, is a sort of discovery that can only be expected in small, off-the-map farms like Brock's Hole; and if the so-called progressive section of the English farming community gets its way, I suppose such small farms will soon be merged into vast collective farms (controlled, if not from Whitehall itself, then at least from some office in the towns), and agriculture will in general become so highly mechanized that horses will be as rare in our farms as golden orioles in our woods, and the Jacks of to-morrow will certainly have no chance to indulge such frivolous fancies as plaits and braids, bells and brasses.

Meanwhile, I may perhaps be allowed to take my fill of pleasure in Brock's Hole while it lasts. It is something if one can say one has enjoyed the savour of such things before they passed completely. Inside the farm-house itself much the same sort of unique atmosphere prevails. Perhaps Priscilla is less lenient than Jack in her attitude towards the way things are going to-day; for she is a woman, tenacious of the past, and almost idolatrously fond of her old father.

I saw her on the green this morning waiting for the 'bus which the recently cleared highroads now enable to run. The service is, to say the best of it, still highly erratic, and Priscilla, when I met her, had already been waiting the best part of an hour. But anybody who, even in normal times, must take so much trouble for the very simplest journey, is not likely to be much upset by a wait of a mere hour or so. She was going to the hospital to visit her father, and the number of parcels and baskets which accompanied her suggested that she was taking the best part of her storeroom with her by way of gratitude for the kind treatment he was receiving.

"One thing he told me to be sure and not forget," she said, "and that was his bread and butter. He says they feed him wonderfully—a lot better than I do!—but he misses my home-made bread and butter."

Priscilla's woollen-hooded face, pinched with cold and glazed with the shine of the reflected snow, creased into a smile of justifiable pride. Every week she bakes her own bread, and her father will eat no other. In fact, he never had eaten any other bread until he went into hospital, and it is one of his little grievances that, owing to the mysterious workings of the wheat quota, he can no longer have his bread made from flour that has been milled from his own home-grown wheat. Priscilla's butter, like her batches of bread, is made for home consumption only: it seems to them, up at Brock's Hole, just plain common sense that, if you farm the land, you should surely be able to get the best part of your food from what that land yields.

Thus it is a matter for continual amusement to Farmer Deeping (mixed, perhaps, with a little amazement) that his brother Paul, who is also a farmer, will insist on bringing his own white shop loaf in his pocket when he comes to pay them a visit. "He says he can't tackle our bread," says Mr. Deeping; "can't get on with it nohow. Which only shows, now doesn't it?"—though what exactly it shows he does not explain.

With her father away in hospital, and Jack, most evenings, somewhere down in the village, Priscilla has need not to be a timid woman. Nevertheless, even she confessed that, since this snowy spell, she has perhaps felt a little lonely at times. I can well believe her. The wind whines through the old house, the snow blows under the locked door, and outside not a single track remains identifiable to link her with the nearest cottage half a mile away.

"I'd have been all right, I think," she says, "if Lady hadn't been ill. I used to hear her coughing out there in the stable, and—well, it wasn't exactly pleasant. I told Jack a dozen times he ought to put an end to her misery; but he wouldn't. He made the excuse that if they shot her, they'd never get her out to the roadway, through all those snowdrifts; but I'm sure it was really because he always was so fond of Lady and couldn't bring himself to believe there wasn't any hope. Anyway, she had to be shot in the end. Yesterday it was; and they got her out into the road easily enough, after all. Dragged her over the snow with the tractor, and she hardly made a mark. Jack said she rode as soft as velvet."

There are days in spring when the sky can be ecstatic over Brock's Hole, so many are the larks that seem to prefer this spot for their special territory. It is as if invisible hands held a crown of singing light over the place: as if this little farm, worked almost entirely by an old father and his two willing children, were somehow preferred above its neighbours. Indeed, for me at any rate, Brock's Hole, while Farmer Deeping lives, is a place apart. I rarely pass that way, whether it is across the fields or between the blackthorn foam of that rutty-green ride, without I pause to lift the wooden bolt out of the barn door and see if the old farmer is pottering about somewhere inside. For the barn is where he seems to spend most of his time these days, as if his weak, narrowing eyes preferred the owlish dusk there to the sharp light in the fields outside. Through the chinks and knot-holes in the barn walls the light falls in soft pencil-rays, mote-filled, and subtly emphasizing the darkness of the interior. And like a shadow the old man dreams among his dusty relics and implements of yesterday.

Few talks have given me greater pleasure, or sent me home more certainly renewed in spirit, than those I have enjoyed with the old man as we sat on the sacks piled up near his threshing-floor. Perhaps "talks" is the wrong word to describe those rich, lazy half-hours; for Farmer Deeping is not much of a talker. He voices no pithy remarks, as Thurston, for instance, does; and if—but this is rare—he should attempt to illustrate his point with a story, the chances are he will either lose sight of the story before he has finished it or he will bring it to such a vague conclusion that you are still left wondering whether he has finished or not. And yet, in spite of this, something valuable is imparted, some fragrance of a life lived in quiet fullness and now drawing to its close. The whole of that life has been devoted, happily and unstintedly, to the land that was his father's before him and should be (but alas, probably will not be allowed to be) his son's after him; and from those forty acres the whole richness of his character springs.

The tractor may be working outside, in the fields, but here, in the barn, the past still holds precarious sway. I think that is perhaps why Farmer Deeping is so often to be found in here. Among the dust and cobwebs on the beams—so hardened with age that a nail will hardly penetrate them—hang such all-but-forgotten farm implements as flails ("frails," as everybody hereabouts calls them), barley hummelers, sickles, and scythes. If you want to unloose the old man's tongue, one almost infallible way is to invite his explanation of the use and practice of such pre-mechanical tools and properties as these. For him they have not yet been reduced to the unkindly status of "relics" or "bygones": indeed, he still occasionally threshes out some beans with a flail, and it is the pride of the year for him when, at the commencement of harvest, he takes down his scythe, hones it, and begins mowing down the corn around the difficult headlands or where it has been badly laid by the weather. The main work of the harvest is Jack's, with his spitting, snorting tractor; but there are still places where the binder is useless, and there the old man and his whistling scythe come into their own.

Over in one corner of the barn stands a dressing-machine, complete with every grade of sieve; and this, too, he contrives sometimes to find a use for. From an economic point of view it may be a waste of time; but the satisfaction it gives to Farmer Deeping to stand there turning the handle that shakes the sieves and rotates the fans and sets the whole box of tricks clattering is not to be measured in terms of economics. It is certainly a tiring job, and the most that can be dressed is about forty quarters a day. Jack laughs and calls it a waste of time, but he is wise enough to keep his laugh and his criticism to himself.

These old tools and implements are the farmer's tangible contact with a day when farming was less a trade than a way of life. Over in another dusty corner of the barn, for instance, stands a hand chaff-cutter. "When Father was alive," the old man said to me one day, as I stood by watching him feed the hay to the cumbersome blade, "there used to be a man come round regularly, with his own little chaff-cutter. He carried it on his back, and went about from place to place, putting in a morning's work here and an afternoon's work there. He didn't do anything else. There was always a meal for him when he came here and he brought us news of friends and farmers we hadn't seen for donkey's years. He used to be as interested in Father's horses and crops as if they were his own. I don't suppose he could have ever earned more than a shilling or two a day, but, oh, he was a happy old man. I can see him now, sitting in the kitchen with one of Mother's pies in front of him, and laughing and talking a good 'un. But now it wouldn't be worth his while, would it? They'd say he took too long; and, anyway, where's the horses to-day?"

Perhaps the thing I like most of all among Farmer Deeping's outmoded stock-in-trade is his winnowing-fan. Made of cane, it is fashioned like a vast scallop shell which, resting on the shoulder-blade, fits perfectly into the bend of the upraised arm when being carried. Its only use now is to collect the chaff, or "small stuff," and carry it away, either from the dressing-machine or from the wasteful heaps left behind by the threshers. Beautiful as a leaf, and as perfectly adapted to its own ends, it is for me the very symbol of that earlier husbandry which was the pride of the English countryside and the decay of which is now our loss and shame. Brock's Hole was just the place in which to find such a treasure; and who better than old Farmer Deeping to go striding across the rickyard with it pitched against his shoulder, laden with chaff that others would leave to rot or blow away?

Unhappy will be the day for England when such men are no longer to be found serving its willing acres!

Chapter Ten

I T is as if the whole round earth beneath our feet had gone dead: as if we were living now on another moon.

I look out of the window into the garden (or where the garden ought to be) and I see none of those comforting rings of bare earth in the snow, as if the plants' warm breath had melted a clearing round their living leaves. The wallflowers and Brompton stocks, which I planted in the autumn, stand out of the snow like grey rags tied to a stick; there is no warm breath in *those* leaves to melt away the snow. And that apple-tree, round whose base there should by now be showing the golden bubbs of the aconite—can such a filigree of iron ever break into a million down-flushed buds? As for the vegetable garden, that spade has not yet been invented which could dig up my leeks or parsnips, frozen into the earth like fossils in a rock. The whole universe has lost its breath; and in this arctic moment it seems to be touch and go whether it will ever find it again.

Mutz died last night, and the only way of burying him this morning was by thawing the ground a little with a bonfire. His death was itself something of a symbol—for me, at least—of the withering cold that has had us all in its grip these last few days. Eight months old, he was still not much more than midway between kitten and cat: a frolicking, irresponsible little creature one minute and already a not quite staid tom the next.

There had seemed nothing whatever wrong with him, no possible reason why he should die. And then yesterday afternoon he suddenly sickened. I made him a warm bed by the fire, and, since he refused all food and drink, left him to sleep. Sleep, I know, will cure most of the ills that cat-flesh is heir to, and so I did not worry. But the sickness increased. Nothing I could do seemed to relieve him; as soon as the bout was over, he would curl up in his rags again, look at me appealingly, and then bury his shivering head.

Once he dragged himself out of his bed, crawled across the floor on sagging legs, and made his way to the saucer in the kitchen where he always has his milk. When he failed to return, I went out to see what had happened, and there he lay in front of his saucer, his mouth inside it, and all the milk spilt over the floor. I warmed and diluted a little; but however much he may have desired it, he was unable to lap it up; and so I carried him back to his bed beside the fire.

I asked where I could for advice, but nobody knew what to suggest. Country cats are expected to look after themselves. "Let him sleep it off," was the general answer to my query; but as the evening advanced, and Mutz continued to lie there, questioning me every now and then, as I imagined, with his dulled eyes (*"Isn't there anything you can do?"*), I found it increasingly difficult to believe that sleep alone would mend all in the end.

To spend one's grief on a dying cat is usually considered a sentimental indulgence, and I admit I have seen instances all too many of people whose grief for suffering animals is only matched by their lack of grief for suffering mankind. "Animals have no souls," says one friend, a Catholic; "and so you do wrong to feel too strongly about the death of a cat." But I find myself preferring the words of another friend: "The virtue of non-attachment is demonstrated daily," he says, "but when creatures of living beauty attach themselves to one, one is willing to sin and take the consequences."

Certainly Mutz was no great beauty. He belonged to that vast,

The lane and the barn

harum-scarum race of country cats whose family tree is as rank as an elder and quite as ineradicable. But equally certainly he knew how to attach himself to one. All the wiles of the cat tribe who, of all living creatures, best know the art of retaining their independence while at the same time flattering the human desire for a show of complete submission, were his *in excelsis*. He gave, only in so far as it pleased him to give; and in return he got—all he wanted! It was impossible (at least in this household) to deny him. From the moment he crossed the threshold, deep in the safety of a jacket pocket, he ruled the place.

Clearly enough, I recall the occasion when we first brought Mutz home. I had asked the baker to try to find me a cat, knowing his own affection for all cats; and apparently all the mongrels of the parish were passed under review before Mutz was discovered and duly pronounced by him as just the cat for me.

It was Heinz's birthday—his first in England after being hounded out of a Nazified Vienna. With all the Austrian's love of animals and birds (did they not once charter an aeroplane to rescue the blizzard-caught swallows, stranded in the Alps, and carry them into the sunshine of the south?) he had asked me to get a kitten. At first I hesitated, remembering Sambo's depredations amongst the birds in my garden. With the skill of a tight-rope walker, Sambo would tread the top of the hedge and pick the naked wretches out of their nests. A family of yellow-hammers, flashing the gold nuggets of their heads in the sun of my garden, is as precious to me as rare flowers are in other gardens, and I did not relish the thought of a second Sambo nullifying my pleasure. And there was another thing. Sambo was a wanderer and had finally paid the price of his freedom by getting himself caught in a rabbit-snare, an end I was not anxious to have repeated.

But cats are not to be denied by mere humane considerations like these. Their persistence is almost psychic: they get themselves a home in spite of the stoutest denials. If there is somebody in the room who hates cats, it is just her lap and none other they will choose, and the unhappy recipient of their attentions has no alternative but to pretend she feels herself honoured. So with Mutz: in spite of all my determination, he arrived—as if the very stars in their courses had ordained it so.

One evening in July, therefore, we walked over to Nat Swift's to fetch him. The way home took us past Charlie Beslyn's cottage. From behind the leafy screen of his garden he must have been watching us; for that night a Woolworth envelope was handed in at my door, addressed in Charlie's clear, untutored hand. Inside were the following verses:

> The primrose path of happiness
>   Is walked in greatest measure
> By those who seek, and find content
>   In simple childlike pleasures.
> This night I saw two men who found
>   Delight, in simple treasure
> By playing with a tiny pet
>   To occupy their leisure.
> Said Bertha who was with me then
>   (I thought I'd better mention)
> Just look at those two men out there
>   And see how great attention
> They're giving to that tiny thing
>   A little ball of fluff
> A kitten small and black and round
>   And yet just big enough
> To give them greater happiness
>   Than tons and tons of pelf
> Or all the pleasures gained by those
>   Who pander to theirselves.

To set Charlie's verses down in a book, like this, in all the cool precision of print, is rather like setting a simple, stay-at-home girl in the glare of stage limelight: the original merit eludes the daze of publicity. I include them nevertheless, for they became part of our pleasure in Mutz henceforth.

Not many kittens have a poem sung over their christening. It is true that Mutz never showed any signs of wanting to live up to the dignity thus thrust upon him: to the end he remained plebeian, one of the masses, a cat whose manners were no better than they should have been, and whose name (bestowed impromptu, when his sex rendered irrelevant the original Mitsi) was the only unusual thing about him.

And now he is dead. Rightly or wrongly, proportionately or disproportionately, his dying affected me considerably. I believe now that the significance of the event was somehow rendered the more emphatic by (I know it sounds ridiculous) the weather. I found it impossible to get warm that night. Even when I sat inside the fireplace, logs and coals conspiring together for my comfort, I found the heat more an illusion than a reality. Somewhere inside me a core of cold persisted. And perhaps because of this, the sight of Mutz, incommunicable in his suffering, shivering his life away in that bundle of rags, bit itself the more keenly into my consciousness.

I tried to read, but the picture of a dying cat imposed itself between me and the words. At midnight, unable to do anything more to relieve him, I piled up the fire, tucked Mutz into his rags, and went upstairs to bed. I tried to sleep, but the thought of a dying cat came between me and the oblivion I sought. Finally, at about two-thirty, weary of the attempt to shut him out of my mind, I came downstairs again.

Never, in England, have I known such intentful cold. It seemed to squeeze the breath out of my body, as if I were being clamped in a relentless vice. Now, I felt, was the very zero hour of all this bitter spell of bad weather. In the fireplace was nothing but a heap of ashes. Mutz had crawled out of his bed and lay on the hearthrug a foot or so away. His eyes were open, but there was no meaning left in them. I lifted his paw. It was still warm, but it fell aimlessly out of my fingers.

I covered him over and went back to bed. And as I lay there, shivering, the fact of his death began to assume almost morbid proportions, until it seemed to focus the evil intensity of the cold. The force I had seen at work in the lane outside, piling up those malignant and yet lovely drifts of snow, so silently and so remorselessly, became for the moment identified for me with the death of my cat.

    Uneasily at last I slept; and when I came down this morning, Mutz's body was frozen fast to the mat.

Chapter Eleven

LARKFIELD is typical of most English villages in that it possesses one fair-sized general stores, where you may buy anything from bacon to wine (the "rich, fruity port" beloved of cottagers), patent medicines to paraffin, or silk stockings to garden implements, and a number of small shops where, on the other hand, the selection is so limited and the service so casual that you may wonder how their owners manage to make a living out of such a twopenny-ha'penny turnover. As a matter of fact, I don't think the owners of most of these small shops, many of which are no more than converted front rooms of cottages, do make a living out of them. I don't think they ever really imagined they would.

Small farmers, whom these competitive times have squeezed out of their farms; craftsmen, who forsook their calling just in time to save some of the little capital it had brought them in better, more honest days; men and women on the look-out for some convenient means of eking out a more than modest income—such are the general run of owners of these little village shops. And if they welcome the pence that come trickling over the counter, it is certain they welcome even more the people who bring those pence. Trade is more an excuse for companionship than a means of livelihood.

If, for instance, you want the nearest Larkfield can give to an efficient, up-to-date service you must go to Mr. Mugridge's shop, where, with a modicum of good luck, you will get what you ask for; for Mr. Mugridge keeps the general stores, and serves the gentry, and draws the main custom of the parish. But if you go to Mrs. Wright's, or Mr. Ley's, or Mrs. Clark's, the goods you pay for over the counter will almost certainly be the least of what you will bring away with you. You buy a pound of sugar from Mrs. Wright —or Mr. Ley, or Mrs. Clark—and a pound of good fellowship is thrown in for make-weight.

Mrs. Wright, in fact, is an excellent example of this pleasant class of small village shopowners. "Shop" is almost too pretentious a word for the blue-washed room in her thatched cottage where she stocks sweets for the children, tobacco and fizzy drinks for the harvesters, and the less perishable groceries for their wives.

A visit to Mrs. Wright invariably entails an inspection of Bessie, the sow, sucking her curly tailed litter as she lies stretched out and snorting in her sty, or a stroll round the garden to see Mr. Wright's marrowfat peas or Mrs. Wright's cabbage roses, not to mention a conversation over the counter that may be productive of anything, from a forthright criticism of the newfangled methods being adopted over at Nortofts Farm to an unrecorded scrap of folk-song, sung in quavering and not-quite-unison by both Mr. and Mrs. Wright, or it may be productive of just nothing but the simple good feeling that accompanies a sincere inquiry after your health or an obvious pronouncement upon the state of the weather.

In days like these, when a knifing wind blows all day unhindered from the North Sea and the snow is a blinding weariness to the eyes, it is good to run into Mrs. Wright's for some trifle which you could probably very well do without. You hurry up the garden path to escape the wind as soon as possible, push open her door, and take shelter inside the friendly little shop.

Perhaps she will ask you through into the room beyond, where Mr. Wright, deaf and difficult, sits over the fire, lighting his pipe with a sere stick of hazel.

Such visits are sometimes productive of the most surprising

scraps of information, for the Wrights both come of farming stock and were themselves farmers long before they became shopkeepers. Photographs are taken out of a drawer, fading snapshots that still reflect a world that soon will be totally forgotten. Here is one of Mrs. Wright sitting up in her gig, neat and trim as a farmer's wife ought to be; and with shy, quiet pride she tells how she spanked along the road, coming home from market, overtaking all the other farmers and their wives on the way. And here is another of Mr. Wright, some fifty years ago, spruce in his suit of corduroy, whip in hand as he stands beside two proud horses hitched to a load of corn which he is taking to be milled. He looks the part all right, smiling out of the faded photograph; but there was evidently some sort of wanderlust calling him, for about this time he left his father's farm, intending to go to sea. With a friend, he somehow made his way to Liverpool.

"It was late at night when we got there," he told me, "and we paid for a room in a dutty ol' place—well, I dunno *who* hadn't slept there afore us. 'I ain't takin' no clothes off here, Jim,' I say, and I slept in all I'd got. Next morning, we were up early and went down to see the ships. I recollect the seat where we sat—one of them iron seats, you know, stuck in the pavement. I hadn't never sen the sea afore, and when I see them big ships on it, a-disappearin' out of sight, I say to Jim, 'Jim, come on! I'm going home. I don't think I want to go to sea after all!'"

When Mr. Wright married and took a farm of his own, I suspect it was mainly his wife who kept things going, just as she still does, when her husband is old and ailing and terribly temperamental. It is true that he has the lowest opinion of her abilities, but I notice he lets her do the work all the same.

"Clackety-clack," he says, "clackety-clack: it's all you ol' wimmen can do!"

And when Mrs. Wright has her sisters, or cousins, in to see her, he is generally to be found pottering around the garden. "You'll find her in there," he says, as I come up the path, and he jerks an impatient thumb over his shoulder, in the direction of the house. "I dessay you can' hear 'em," he adds, bitterly.

Yet I think, after all, it is largely his deafness which causes this impatience with his womenfolk. He suspects, and quite rightly, that they purposely don't let him hear all they are saying. And so he must needs find some way of counteracting this enforced inferiority. So he storms at his old wife on occasion, and, whilst letting her do the work, complains at the way she does it.

Only the other day they gave me an amusing instance of the fact that it is undoubtedly Mrs. Wright, herself white-haired and tottery with rheumatism, who "wears the trousers."

I found them both in the shop and still eager with the excitement of the nocturnal adventure that had befallen them.

"We heard such a thump and a bang in the night," said Mrs. Wright. "It sounded like——" and then, at a loss for the right illustration, she looked round the shop for something to bang with. But Mr. Wright, sensing her difficulty, got in first. He thumped his fist on the trestle counter, so that all the bottles of sweets jumped into the air. "Yes," Mrs. Wright affirmed, "it was even louder than that." "Well, I'm deaf," chimed in Mr. Wright, "but I heard it clear enough. We sat up in bed and Missus she lighted the candle. It was half-past two. 'Lawk-a-mussy,' I said, 'what's that?'" "I was sure there was somebody downstairs," said Mrs. Wright, taking up the thread of the story and holding it. "We listened and listened, but we couldn't hear anything. Then at half-past three we said we'd go downstairs and see what it was. Tom was all for getting his gun." "'I'll shoot 'un,' I said," Mr. Wright continued, the male in him seizing the opportunity for self-aggrandizement. "Of course, I wouldn't only a-shot 'un in the leg. But Missus, she said, 'No, don't shoot 'un; I'll take your stick with me.' And I followed her down the stairs." "We looked everywhere with the candle," said Mrs. Wright, claiming as hers the cadence and conclusion of the tale, "but we couldn't see anything anywhere. . . . And just now I found out what it was. A brick had fallen through the ceiling in the spare room: it must have come unlodged from the chimney-stack somewhere. But my, it did give us a jump!"

An hour they had sat there in the candlelight, still as mice, debating in whispers what to do; and then (I'm sure Mr. Wright in his excitement never guessed what confession had escaped him) it was Mrs. Wright, incapable, talkative female as she was, who led the way downstairs, stick in hand, to face the enemy.

Only in one matter will Mr. Wright never allow his wife to meddle. She may look after the shop, she may feed the fowls, she may even shift the fowls from one run to another (though, of course, she does so under a hail of criticism: "Drat the woman, she ain't got no more sense than a rabbit!"), she may attend to the garden, and she may gather in the plums and apples; but feed and tend the pig she may not.

If ever I see Mrs. Wright stumbling round the sty, in that bygone coat of hers, long-skirted and puff-sleeved, I know that Mr. Wright must be ill. For Bessie the sow is sacrosanct to her master's special care. She is child to him. She is everything to him.

When he is compelled to remain upstairs, he can overlook the sty from his bed, and Mrs. Wright knows, as she unbolts the gate and takes the pail of swill into the scared animal, that her every action is being closely watched. And when the doctor says he may get up again, and perhaps go out in the sun a little, the first thing he does is to wander down the garden to Bessie and commune with her over the fence.

If Bessie herself is ill, whatever the hour and whatever the expense, the vet must be fetched; and more than once I have had Mrs. Wright on my doorstep, coppers ready in hand, pleading for me to telephone to the town for help.

"Tell him he *must* come," she says. "Mr. Wright is in a rare state about Bessie. Tell him he *must* come."

And recently, when the shortage of animal foodstuff was at its worst and cottage pigs and hens were being killed off wholesale, because a short-sighted Government had failed to realize that in wartime it might be difficult to get supplies from abroad, Mrs. Wright must have spent many weeks' profits from sweets and sugar and ginger-beer in an endeavour to get food for the precious sow.

The reason for this almost religious attitude towards Bessie is written in bold white paint over the door. THOMAS WRIGHT. PORK BUTCHER. LICENSED SLAUGHTER-HOUSE FOR PIGS. Inside, there is more evidence of the reason. From the whitewashed beams of the ceiling hang a "spreader" and a couple of gigantic hooks. Over in one corner of the lean-to is a salting tub of immense proportions. And part of an elm-tree-trunk, four feet in diameter, stands in another corner. Spiders spin their webs from the "spreader" and the cutting-up block is used for a mere table, and the tub holds only Mrs. Wright's supply of soft washing water; but once they all had a nobler use.

For miles around Mr. Wright was famed for his sausages and his home-cured hams—particularly his sausages. People speak of them even to-day with a delight and longing that suggest their savour still lingers on the palate.

Village carpenters, as I have already suggested, are sometimes immortalized in the field-gates they made; blacksmiths in window-latches, oven doors, and the like; whilst many a thatcher's work is pointed to with pride long after he is dead. Mr. Wright's immortality will be in the memory of the sausages he made. So long as any man lives who once upon a time tasted them, he will not be forgotten.

His hams graced the table up at the Hall. Indeed, he still receives an occasional supply of pork from there to cure in his own inimitable fashion; but his criticism of the way it is cut and his chagrin that he can no longer do the whole business from A to Z combine to make the job no more than a half-hearted one—a sour reminder of past, irrevocable glories. And his pork-cheeses (nothing will induce him to call them brawn) were a delicacy enjoyed far beyond this parish. But his proper pride was in his sausages alone.

He knew their worth and he knows it still, and I verily believe he would think it neither immodest nor irreligious if the fact should be commemorated on his tombstone.

Meanwhile, that blistered bit of board over his door is a sufficient memorial. Mr. Wright has not killed a pig for years, but every March he still pays for his licence to be renewed. "Just in case," he says, in defence of the extravagance; but I have a shrewd idea it is solely that he may continue to keep that notice nailed over his doorway.

Pagan warriors treasure the scalps of their enemies and wealthy horticulturists point with pleasure to some rare gentian fetched from the High Alps; and why should not Mr. Wright be allowed the gesture of that bit of board over his door to commemorate the day he made sausages of such wide repute?

With such a reputation singing in his shiny old head, no wonder if he sits back now and lets the women do the work. Something may surely be allowed, even in this feminist age, for the dignity of manhood! *His* work is done. Things must go on, it is true; ordinary, everyday things like feeding fowls and serving fizzy drinks; but let the women look after these. . . . So he concentrates on Bessie and lets most of the rest go by. How long Mrs. Wright will continue to be able to cope with all the work that falls on to her sloping shoulders seems not to bother him: nor, if appearances are anything to go by, does it bother her. She has the blessed ability of taking everything as it comes.

To watch Mrs. Wright out in the garden these days of bitter weather, feeding the fowls, is scarcely to be set thinking of the village beauty. Her puff-sleeved coat is buttoned high round the neck. Her vast tam-o'-shanter flops over her white hair. And she treads as if her feet were bare to the spiky ice. Yet it is clear, on closer view and in rare moments of unmitigated health and happiness, that she could once have set men staring after her as she strode along. It does not need those faded photographs to assure one of the truth of this. I dared to say as much to her one day, as she paused in serving me, and some play of light from the window restored the beauty of her mobile face; but she only smiled a moment shyly, a little sadly, then looked away and said, "Maybe!"

I think her happiest days were when, together, they farmed Woodlands Farm and she drove home from market on Wednesday evenings, flicking her whip, and gaily calling out to the friends she overtook. Why they ever gave up the farm at all I have never rightly understood. The natives have their own ideas on the subject, but it is not always wise to accept their interpretation of private tragedies. From driving your own smart gig to market to driving a few old hens from one run to another is a long journey, and it has told heavily on Mrs. Wright. Her courage, however, has seen her through, and, to the outside world at least, she gives no hint of possible cankers eating at the heart of things.

It was one of the soldiers serving with the local searchlight unit who, the other day, set me pondering about the pride (he called it obstinacy and worse) of such small village shopkeepers as Mrs. Wright.

"There's no sense in it," he said. "You go into their shop and ask for something. They haven't got it and they won't be bothered to get it. They don't care whether they serve you or not. Dammit, what do they keep their shop for?"

It had happened to him, he said, times out of number during the five months he had been stationed in Larkfield, and he was reluctantly forced to the conclusion that, of all the inhabitants, and he hadn't a terribly high opinion of any of them, these small shopkeepers, petty tradesmen as he called them, were the laziest of the lot.

"You'd think they would be only too glad of the extra custom the war brings them—to say nothing of the fact that, after all, we did leave decent jobs and come here to defend 'em. But no, they don't give a tinker's cuss for extra custom; and when they do serve you with anything, they adopt a take-it-or-leave-it attitude that just gets my goat."

Wild Campion

But the soldier, I think, had got the matter a little bit askew. It is true enough that he left a good job, and all the comfort it implied, to do what he considered his duty; and it is also true that this duty has so far meant little else but almost unmitigated boredom in a camp that became waterlogged almost as soon as it was occupied and has been snowed under ever since. But what does that mean to Mrs. Wright?

Frankly, so far this war is something that is happening quite outside her ken. Certainly it will be a different matter when the bombs begin to fall; but at the moment she has not the faintest idea what it is all about.

The aeroplanes roar overhead, the searchlights fence the night sky with javelins of fire, there are a few soldiers in the village, there are ration-cards and black-outs and air-raid wardens; but these all belong to a scheme of things of which she has but the vaguest comprehension.

I stood in her garden with her the other day, while she was scattering corn to the fowls. A dispatch-rider flashed by on his motor-cycle, noisy and urgent on some errand of war. A bomber sped over the snow-blackened skies, returning—who knows?—from some deathly mission over the North Sea. Mrs. Wright heeded neither of them. She just went on scattering corn while the eager hens clustered round her feet. The dispatch-rider and the bomber meant next to nothing to her: they were totally outside the realities that have made up the seventy years of her quiet, courageous life.

And that night I happened to come upon a passage in Stephen Spender's *September Journal*. "Above all," the poet writes, "the world should be home, it should be somewhere where everyone has his place, is surrounded by the simple machinery, the task, the house, the furniture, the companion, the river, the trees or streets which assure him that he is loved. Everything should be rooted. This is the simplest thing in life, it is the cocoon that surrounds childhood, it is the simple security of the flesh and the kiss and the fireplace and the setting sun which brings him home.

"No one should want anything except to find his place in life, the centre of his potentiality to love and be loved. Yet if love is the essential thing in life, loss of it is the fiend which enters certain bodies and tears the life around them into shreds. The depredations of the loveless and the homeless who seek power over their fellow beings, can be seen everywhere to-day. The world suffers from the worst and least necessary of mental illnesses—homesickness. The papers are filled with photographs, and have been for years, of those who have been driven out of their homes—the endless rustle of shuffling peasant feet through the dust all night along the road outside Malaga, the family with their possessions piled up on a cart outside a burning Polish farm-house, the widow searching amongst the ruins of her house for a souvenir. They are driven from the little hole which surrounded and comforted them, into the elemental world of alien stones and light. Most homeless of all, little shreds of matter from distant countries that have nothing to do with them, are driven through their flesh. The whole universe of Outside enters their bodies—a fragment of a bomb, a bullet."

And I thought at once of Mrs. Wright, scattering her corn to the silly fowls, while the dispatch-rider flashed past and the bomber hurled through the clouds overhead. May that day never come when she, too, joins those nameless thousands of the homeless ones— a widow searching amongst the ruins of her house for a souvenir.

The soldier, however, was not only wrong in imputing to such as Mrs. Wright too vivid a perception of the war and what it entailed; he was also wrong in his estimate of what he called their obstinacy.

I did not tell him, but that same day I had seen an easy example of the kind of thing he complained about. Some threshers had been at work in a rickyard near by. Cold as it was, they had gone to Mrs. Wright for some of her fizzy drinks; but she had run out of them. In fact, crates of empty bottles have stood about the shop for weeks, waiting for the manufacturer's van to collect them. That afternoon she asked me to telephone and see what was the matter. Would they please explain why they had not been near the place for nearly two months and would they ask the van to call next Thursday, as it always used to? They promised; but of course on Thursday the van never arrived. I suggested to Mrs. Wright that she should send them an order by post: perhaps, with the order in front of them, they would remember to call.

"No," she replied, "I shan't do anything more about it. They'll turn up one day and then I'll let 'em see that I can be just as independent as they can. If they don't want to serve me, they needn't. I can quite well manage without."

And manage without she will. Never mind if there are a hundred and one reasons (illness, for instance, or shorthandedness, or what she calls "this war business") why the fizzy drinks never arrived. Never mind if she has to say no to all the thirsty threshers and roadmen and cyclists who may come panting into the shop. She will have lost her trade but she will have kept her pride.

And that, I think, is just the point which the soldier did not quite realize. At all costs Mrs. Wright will keep her pride. And it is the same with most small shopkeepers. Pride, we are told, is one of the deadly sins; but suppose it means pride in that little freedom which is all one has?

It is the job of shopkeepers to serve, and in serving they too often become servile. There is nothing servile about Mrs. Wright, however; and she, in common with Mr. Ley and Mrs. Clark and all the other cottage shopkeepers in the parish, does not sell you her freedom when she sells you her tobacco and groceries.

In this she differs from the larger shopkeepers. In the days before shopping by post and free delivery within a fifty-mile radius, the gentry did at least a fair proportion of their shopping in the village. Not to do so would have seemed to them unpatriotic. And so, when the Hall carriage drove up before the local general stores, there was a sudden commotion inside, and the grocer, hastily wiping his hands on his stiff white apron, flew out of the door, bowed, and, paper in hand, stood there in the wind and the cold, jotting down her ladyship's order. With a jingle the carriage drove away and the grocer returned to his duties, slightly flushed and confused from so near a contact with the great ones of this world. That sort of thing has gone on for generations until the whole race of large village shopkeepers has become tainted, however decreasingly, with the odour of servility. It is in their blood.

But it is not in the small shopkeeper's blood, since, as he did not benefit by her ladyship's patronage, neither did he have to pay for it in terms of servility.

Hence, therefore, Mrs. Wright's "obstinacy." She will sell you what she has got, but she will not necessarily go out of her way to sell you what she has not got. Particularly if you are a "foreigner." Half of her merchandise is good fellowship and, as such, only to be bought by those with whom she is truly familiar. What the soldier was up against was not so much obstinacy as the fact that he was, after all, a stranger.

Perhaps that day is not far off now when these small village shops will have gone the way of so much more that used to give the countryside its quiet, leisurely character and its sterling worth. Just as the big farms are swallowing up the small farms, so the big shops will swallow up the small shops. Rapidly we see the omnivorous mastication going on already. The war has delayed the process. We are learning to rely more on what we can get at home. And this isolating snow has even further centred us on the immediate community in which we dwell. But the process is only delayed, no more. We may have glimpses to-day of what village life was like when it was its own self-supporting entity; but they are no more than glimpses, soon to be lost again.

If I should be living in Larkfield when this process of mastication is completed, and Mrs. Wright's shop, and Mr. Ley's, and Mrs. Clark's, and all the rest of them have reverted to the domestic cottages they once were, I do not suppose there will be much compensation in the fact that I can remember the time when shopping could be as much a social visit as a commercial transaction.

Still, perhaps it is better to have shopped like this once than never to have shopped like this at all; and when efficiency rules, even in the remotest hamlets, it will perhaps be something to make the young folk goggle when one can tell of summer evenings when one went shopping at Mrs. Wright's, and found her sitting in the garden on an old form lodged against the plum-trees, the setting sun in her eyes and her hands quietly folded in her lap, and sat down beside her and listened to the idle talk, like a woodland stream lapping against the stones, till one forgot what one had come for and went home again, a full hour later, empty-handed (unless with a gift of fruit or new-laid eggs) but far from empty-hearted.

Chapter Twelve

OVER in High Wood the gamekeeper walks through the avenues of young spruces, bringing food to his pheasants. It is against the rules and regulations, in wartime, to feed partridges and pheasants, I believe, but in that case all I can say is Peel is not the only man whom this hard weather has forced into disobedience.

Out of the level whiteness, pocked with the dint of bird-prints and here and there a spatter of blood, melodramatic on the bright snow, the spruces rise in exact formation, less a wood than a regiment of trees. Hooded with snow, like the soldiers fighting in Finland, they thrust out white-gloved hands from which, every now and then, a snow-bomb falls, with an explosion that shatters the wood's intensified quiet.

These are hard days for Peel's birds and hard days for Peel himself. Though the pheasants are standing up to the weather fairly well, the partridges are dying off daily. It is true that he would be feeling their loss more than he does were it not for the fact that Squire only gave two shoots last season and therefore the birds could afford a bit of thinning out.

In the end war's effects are mainly considered in so far as they touch our own lives and our own work; and Peel's chief grudge against Hitler's precipitation of hostilities so far is that it has completely disorganized those shoots that are the aim and end of all his labour.

"I've got some wonderful birds," he says; "but what's the use? Squire says I'll have to shoot 'em myself: a pretty how-de-do, eh?"

Four thousand acres is the extent of the Squire's estate and to Peel this is all one gigantic sanctuary for his birds. Everything and anything that mitigates against a successful breeding season—foxes, wars, badgers, poachers, and so on—is his enemy. He almost seemed to take the view, last September, that Hitler might at least have waited until the shooting season was over before he began upsetting things as he did. In this, however, I must confess that he is only adopting the same point of view as many who had not even his excuse, namely, that gamekeeping, after all, was his livelihood. To many a hunting and shooting man and woman the Führer was a spoil-sport: is not their whole year little more than a crescendo of waiting until autumn announces the opening of the season?

Perhaps Peel was already a little spoiled the year before last, when suddenly Larkfield awoke to find itself the centre of Army manoeuvres. The quiet lanes shook with the rattle of lorries, engineers overran gardens and fields with tangles of telephone wires, guns were fired on the green, blowing windows and ceilings down and frightening the sick and aged almost out of their wits. Only the Squire's breeding woods were immune from this harsh invasion. Large W.D. notices appeared, nailed to the trunks of convenient trees, forbidding the firing of guns or the intrusion of the Army in general. Old women might have their wits blown to pieces, apparently, but the Squire's birds must not be disturbed.

And although I never taxed Peel about it, I am confident he was in hearty agreement with such a privileged scheme of things, nor saw anything ironical in those W.D. notices so prominently displayed upon his trees.

And indeed, why should he? He served in the last war, and, as his frequent stories show, was given plenty of evidence of the sacrosanct status of the sportsman, whether in civvies or in uniform.

"Some of the officers in our battalion," he said, "bet as I wouldn't bring down a buzzard. It was when we were occupying the Rhineland. Well, I bought a gun from a German for 200 marks —and marks was 190 to the pound, then. And another thing: bullets were iron and not lead. Still, I got up early one morning and off I went down to the river with that old gun. I'd had my eye on a particular buzzard there for several days. I waited and then presently along she came—flying lovely she was, easy as a glider. I fired once, and missed. Now I've lost her, I thought. But I fired again, and brought her down. My, weren't they pleased when I took that buzzard into the mess after breakfast! Of course it was all against orders to shoot buzzards, but that was winked at all right. Still, there wasn't half a shindy when I took the bird into Cologne, later, to have it stuffed."

I have always detested gamekeepers—or, rather, I always used to detest them. Brought up in a woodland countryside, I looked upon them as the evil spirits of those haunted, delightful places.

As some people love the sea, so I loved, and always have continued to love, the woods. I would wander off alone and stay for hours in the depths of the woods, whether they were thickets of tangled brier and hazel, where the nightingale sings in the heat of noon—louder, finer, than he ever sings under cover of the velvet darkness of the night—or tall beechwoods, where the light was green, aqueous, like being under the sea. The woods were friendly to me, places where, if I kept still enough and had patience enough, I could come closer than anywhere else to the secret life of animal and bird. From the ant-hills among the hot drifts of sere pine-needles, where the myriad community hurried to and fro on its mysterious errands, to the birds in the tree-tops, whose songs seemed to my childish mind the very articulation of all that swinging, surging, sunny turbulence of green leaves, I loved the life of the woods.

And what incredible surprises they would suddenly spring at one! How should I ever forget, for instance, that morning when, straying into a woodland territory I had not hitherto explored, I dramatically found myself in an open stretch of first-year hazel and chestnut, where wild lilies of the valley, frailer than our garden species, grew in great quantities, hiding their white-and-green washed bells among the silken banners of their leaves? I had never seen wild lilies of the valley before. And, as if this were not enough, while I stood staring down at the flowers round my feet, nightingales broke into song near by, with those passionate alternations of indrawn breath, like a self-inflicted wound, and full, rapturous phrases, like a release after pain. Lilies and nightingales! Happily, I was too young to do more than accept it all just as it was, too young to moralize away the best part of what I was enjoying: I only knew it was good to be alive!

Yes, I loved the woods and there was only one thing that could overshadow my happiness as I walked in them: the gamekeeper. It was so then, and to a certain extent it has been so for years afterwards. The sight of the gamekeeper in his fawn jacket, long-skirted and bulging with who knows what dead creature, his gun over his shoulder, and his bright, suspicious eyes, seemed to me an intrusion of something very like evil in the last place where I might wish to encounter it.

Somewhere at the back of my mind, I suppose, every time I have come upon a gamekeeper, was the grim memory of a keeper's gibbet, or larder, in a wood at home, where stoats and weasels hung head downwards from an horizontal ash-pole, along with magpies and jays, their gay wings wet and broken and infested with the insects that batten upon decay. I knew this was the keeper's doing and I hated him for it. The picture of that senseless gibbet, as I first saw it, suddenly turning the corner of some sunny, green ride in the woods, printed itself indelibly on my child-mind and remained there to stigmatize all gamekeepers henceforth. The mere fact that they were gamekeepers was good enough for me: as such they were necessarily excluded from any possibility of being other than hateful men, destroyers, parasites on the idle rich, wanton killers, and so forth. I hated them all.

With glove and bill-hook

Until I met Peel. Peel taught me some sort of perspective in the matter; and if I am still not enamoured of gamekeepers as a race, I am at least prepared to accept the logic of their position and to believe that there are others besides Peel who occupy that position, admittedly a difficult one, with some dignity and a good deal of character.

In fact, gamekeepers, I have since decided, are a somewhat maligned and much-suffering people. Their job is about as difficult as any in the parish, since the natural inclination of everybody, short of the Squire himself and his friends, is to be against them. The village policeman's task is simple by comparison. He at least has right on his side, in so far as not even the most rebellious villagers would deny the usefulness of his purpose as the keeper of the peace. But the keeper of the Squire's pheasants and partridges, in most villagers' eyes, serves no such useful purpose.

In this hard winter, for instance, many cottagers have felt the pinch of cold and hunger; and nothing so sharpens a sense of injustice as an empty belly and a meagre grate. Yet these same hungry, cold cottagers must watch the Squire's pheasants impudently stroll about their gardens and allotments, nor lift a finger against them, since, if they do so, the keeper may have the law of them. It is an elementary point of justice but none the less cogent for that.

Mark Thurston put the matter neatly, according to his point of view, in the tap-room of the Wheatsheaf on the morning after the Squire's last shoot. Some of the men present in the pub had money in their pockets to burn: they had put in a day's beating. Moreover, they had obviously enjoyed themselves, though their part in the day's sport had been a menial one. Perhaps Mark, who in his younger days had also enjoyed the exhilaration of a day's beating with the guns, was a little envious that he should now be excluded. And yet I do not altogether think so. Age has bestowed on Mark somewhat of the philosophic mind, and he sees many things to-day in a light that was denied to him yesterday.

"I know the shoots up at tha Hall ain't what they used to be," he said. "Why, I can remember the day—and so can Ben here, if he's a mind to—when two wagons weren't enough to carry home all the birds they shot. Yet if you or me was to see an ol' cock pheasant a-peckin' at our peas one morning and put a bit of salt on his tail—never you mind how!—we could be fined for it, and heavy too. It wouldn't count for nothin' for you to plead that you was hungry (let alone the loss of your peas and all the blessed trouble you took over 'em). That bird ain't your'n, you'd soon be told; and like as not, it'll be the Squire hisself, or one of his pals up there on the bench, as would tell you so. I can't see it's right; I can't, and I never shall.

"Mind you," Mark continued, forestalling a criticism he no doubt sensed was forming itself behind the smiles of some of his audience; "mind you, I'd be a liar if I was to say I hadn't never tasted pheasant-pie meself. I have and I hope I'll live to taste it agen. But that ain't neither here nor there. If Peel was to catch me, I'd be for it; and that's what riles me."

"That's right enough," said Ben, anxious to add his mite to the argument, anxious, also, to share something of the limelight: "it's just like Mark says. I'll tell you what: if I was to set a trap for a rabbit—and they're varmin, ain't they?—and break off its leg an' leave it in the trap a-yellin' all the bloomin' night, folks as had a mind to could get the law on me. So they could. All right then; but if the gentry has a day's shootin', why is it I can't get the law on *them* for leavin' half-shot pheasants to crawl about the fields for days till they die at last in somebody's ditch? It ain't fair, and nobody in his senses can say it is."

Most of the farm-hands find it unfair. Whatever their feelings for the Squire as a person, they feel that in this matter of pheasants and partridges there is somehow one law for them and another for him.

Perhaps it isn't a very strong feeling to-day, and certainly it is stronger in the old men than in the young. Mark and Ben knew Larkfield in the days when the poverty of the farm-labourer (ten shillings a week if they were lucky, anything up to fourteen in a family, and bread and beer as the mainstay of their diet) was something the present generations can scarcely conceive; and stored in their canny old heads are memories of poaching exploits, undertaken out of a necessity which none but a brutal inhumanity could deny, and the cost of which, in fine or imprisonment, was out of all proportion to the offence.

And even these younger members of the community, to whom such exploits are in the main only hearsay, inherit something of the antagonism which colours Mark's and Ben's words. Like the inherited instincts that prompt the behaviour of a swarm of bees or a flock of migrant birds, these inherited memories of the war-to-the-death between poacher and gamekeeper dwell in the mass-mind of the village, prompting its attitude, even to-day.

The grievance against all keepers has its roots deep in our undemocratic past. Poor Peel must bear on his broad shoulders the hates and antagonisms of men long since dead and buried.

I remember very well the day I first had my eyes opened as to the possible humanity of this abhorred race of men. I had been walking through Squerry's Wood one day in spring, when the clearings, forsaken now by the wood-cutters whose faggots lay about in neat piles, were full of windflowers and oxlips and blue dog-violets. I sat against an oak, letting the warm sunlight seep through my pores. I was aware of nothing save the sunshine and the profusion of spring flowers which Dis had scattered round my feet. Such days are rare in the early year and this was the one place in which to spend them. War had not even been reckoned with as a possible solution to the accumulating problems that were vexing Europe: it was those days when we came as near to peace as we ever came between the cataclysm of one war and the next. And to the last speck of me I was happy.

Suddenly I heard feet approaching, snapping the dry twigs under nailed boots. I looked up and saw the familiar figure of the gamekeeper—the leather leggings, the long-skirted coat, the ash stick, and the sack-pockets swinging against the hips. If it had been anybody else, I should have taken no notice; but I suppose that old memory of the bird-hung larder sprang alive in me at the sight of the keeper coming towards me over the blue and white tapestry of the flowers. It acted like a button that sets an alarm bell ringing. I privately wished him to the devil.

"Good afternoon," he said: "I only wanted to say would you mind keeping to the paths and rides just now. You see, my birds are nesting and I don't want them disturbed."

I do not quite know how, but the reasonableness of his request and the hint of a smile that played over his austere features so triumphed over my mood of resentment that I somehow found myself offering him a cigarette!

Another keeper, perhaps, or another way of saying things, and I should almost certainly have made some foolishly sarcastic reply that referred to his precious, pampered birds. Instead, here we were, smoking cigarettes and talking, he leaning against a tree and me with my legs stretched out among the myriad waving flowers. And for that conversion to sweet reasonableness I shall always be grateful to Peel.

For he thereby not only cleared my mind of one of its more obstinate prejudices, but he also prepared the way for many a profitable and enjoyable walk and talk in the future. I came to see that the gamekeeper was not necessarily the evil spirit of the woods I had always imagined him to be. True, even Peel never quite completed my conversion, for not all keepers are Peels. We grow like the thing that most occupies our attention, it is said: butchers are often red-faced and bloody, bakers white as uncooked dough, a rabbit-fancier will look like a rabbit, and a horsy-minded person like a horse, whilst even a gardener imbibes a philosophic calm from his fruitful occupation. So with gamekeepers: as a rule, the animal is all too apparent in their faces. No, Peel has not wholly purged me of my prejudice, but he has at least taught me a measure of common sense in the matter.

Peel knows his woods like the palm of his hand. He knows the intricate paths and rides threading through them. He knows the favourite haunts of the animals that live in them, and he knows their calls and their prints. The woods are his world. To say that he is fond of them is to impute perhaps too conscious a feeling; but, at any rate, there is no other job for which he would exchange this dawn-to-dusk work in the woods and fields.

His knowledge is such as a trained naturalist might well envy; but it was his attitude towards his job that first intrigued me. I soon saw that it is not so much a matter of venom as I had supposed, but an exercise of deeply rooted sportsmanship. In trapping and shooting, he is pitting his cunning against the equal cunning of the birds and animals; and that is what gives him pleasure. His own birds may be pampered—he even admits as much—but his job is to safeguard them against their enemies—"strangers," as he calls them.

Badgers, for instance, may have all the virtues—and more—which the naturalists ascribe to them. They may be clean to the point of finickiness, they may clear the place of docks and beetles, they may be wonderful handy at scratching out bees' and wasps' nests, and their grease may be the sovereign remedy against the "old man"; but for all that they are strangers, they are the enemies of his birds, eating their eggs, and they must go.

Peel will spend days tracking a badger before he is able to spring it. I remember particularly his excitement at a kill last year. All that early spring he tracked the badger's pads, and by their size he knew that he was up against something worth reckoning with.

"She comes along Wally's Lane," he said, "across the field in front of Mill Cottage, over the road there, along the Bottoms, and then where do you think she goes? Somewhere through the orchard alongside my cottage: bloody cheek, eh? A full five miles' trek every night and goodness knows what she does it for. But I'll spring her yet."

And then one day he called me into his garden. Incongruous

and pathetic among the litter of Mrs. Peel's tin baths and pots and the children's broken toys, lay the badger—as stalwart a creature as ever padded over English fields. Her body lay limp along the cobbles, the black and white bristles dead and lustreless.

"I told you I'd spring her," Peel said; "and there she is! And it took pretty nigh an Atlantic cable to catch her, too."

He has the sportsman's admiration for a valiant enemy. Indeed, I suspect it is this rather than any very firm conviction that the badger is outrageously opposed to his own interests that gives him most pleasure in outwitting it.

"Father had a tame badger once, called Sally," he told me. "He kept her on a brace and she was as knowing a customer as ever you saw. Us kids used to think no end of Sally. Then I remember one day mother took ill and we had to send for the doctor. He was a sporting sort of a chap, very handy with a gun. When he came out of the house, after he'd been in to mother, he noticed Sally in the paddock. Father and he fell to talking about badgers as fighters and the doctor said he'd like to set his terrier on to Sally to see what'd happen. He thought a lot of his terrier, did the doctor. So next time he came along he brought the dog with him, and Joan, his daughter. He was dead set on seeing that fight. Father warned him what would happen but he only laughed: he was a rare one for a bit of sport. Go ahead then, father said; and that terrier was dead in a couple of minutes. Sally tore it to ribbons. My, the doctor was surprised—he thought his dog could stand up to anything. And Joan, I remember she cried like a baby."

We were walking through Lordship Wood when Peel told me this story. My inexpert eye had failed to notice a noose of wire among the brambles tangling over the path. It was a badger-trap. The noose was attached to a bent sapling, secured ready to spring at a touch. When Peel had explained the trap to me, he told me about Sally, and then went on to tell of how one moonlight night he had stood waiting against a tree close by a badger's hole. Soon two badgers came out and Peel saw the fight of his life, right there under his eyes, so still he stood in the moonlight, like a bough of the tree.

"They made enough noise to split your ear-drums," he said; "and then, when I'd seen all I wanted, I put a shot through one—but the other got away."

Every now and then, during the course of a walk, Peel will stoop down, without breaking the thread of his talk, rake a few sods away from a mole-trap, knock out a broken-backed mole with a click, and tuck the sleek-coated creature into the deep pockets of his coat.

I asked him if all woodland creatures were his enemies?

"Not by any manner of means," he replied. "Quite a lot of the small birds, for instance, are very useful to me in my job. I'll tell you for why. Say I hear a wren—and you know what a devil of a fuss a wren can kick up for such a small bird? Well, that's probably a cat on the prowl somewhere. Or maybe I hear a blackbird give that warning cry of his, and I know there's a stoat up to no good. I've only got to hear it making a certain cry—I know exactly how—and I go along and make a little whining noise, like so; then up comes the stoat, standing on its hind legs—and that's just the time to catch him! But perhaps the bird that helps most is the starling. It makes more pother than all the other birds put together; and ten to one that means a hawk. Probably a sparrow-hawk. And you know if there's one thing I like to take a pot at more than another it's a sparrow-hawk. They're proper brutes, they are: steal eggs by the hundred."

Peel's best friends, however, are apparently his ferrets.

"I treat my ferrets kind," he will say; "for they work hard for their keep, so the little beggars do. You could put one of my ferrets in your shirt and it wouldn't leave a scratch. Why, one day my youngest kid—she's four—went up the top of the garden and (I dunno how she managed it) but she opened the hutches and let all the ferrets out. And the next thing missus saw was our little Susie with them ferrets all round her legs, running about, and sniffing at her bare flesh; and they didn't leave a mark anywhere."

It was one of Peel's really unlucky days when his favourite ferret lost an eye. He put her in a hole, gave her a flick with his finger, and said, "Up you go!" There was a screaming inside the hole, and when the ferret came out she had one eyeball hanging by a sinew. A fox had bitten it clean out.

"So I got out my knife," said Peel, "and I cut the eyeball away; and there she is in her hutch now, good for many a day's work yet!"

Indeed, it's an odd mixture, the gamekeeper's life. More like a sport, perhaps, than a job of work. It is true that he still buys his pleasure at the expense of a certain ingrained animosity on the part of the rest of the villagers; but at least to-day he is immune from that degree of peril which old Mrs. Dickson referred to, when she told me how her scrapbook of verses had consoled her through long nights during which she had never known if her man would return alive or dead.

There is a lonely farm on the outskirts of Larkfield where, until recent years, a notice was nailed to a tree at the corner of the woodlands: Man Trap, Beware! And the grim engine itself hangs to-day on the farmer's outhouse wall.... But the use of such things is not within the memory of men still living: the present-day keeper knows nothing of the ferocity that was once integral with his work.

Even the gamekeeper's cottage, that stands with its back to the open pastures and its eyes to the thick dusk of the woods, is untenanted now, here as in many another parish. Peel's wife would not live in such a secretive place for twice his present earnings, and Peel himself doesn't much fancy it. Instead, he lives close by the highroad, like anybody else. Nevertheless, he is a man apart, even to day: he is in the parish and yet somehow hardly of it....

"Do you want to see a pretty sight?" he asked me one day in May, when the crab-trees spilled their pink petals on the pasture and every roadside was frothing over with the bloom of kexes.

And in a remote corner of High Wood, where a sandy bank fronted the afternoon sun, we watched some fox cubs playing under the roots of an elm, six or seven of them, innocent as kittens, tumbling and rolling and jumping over one another, blinking in the sunlight, chasing dead leaves, lithe as panthers, and shy as shadows, while the dog and vixen watched from the thicket near by.

"Now if that ain't a pretty thing to see," said Peel, as we came away, "I dunno what is."

And his voice was a shade gentler than usual, his eyes a gleam brighter.

Chapter Thirteen

COUNTRY talk has a flavour of its own when it comes from the lips of men and women whose whole lives have been given in the service of the land. The smell of growing things is in it and the tang of air that blows out of unsullied skies. It is vulgar with the vulgarity of life itself and painted with the poetry of earth. Unless education has spoiled it, robbing it of the vitality that was its well-spring, it carries the history of ages and links this year of grace with the eras of Celt and Saxon long centuries dead.

And the countryside will be the poorer, by the loss of one of its most precious characteristics, when the printed word and the broadcast word, between them, have reduced all its rainbow colours to the common drab of schoolman's speech.

Indeed, it is beginning to be at a discount already. The bilingual Welsh and Irish are not more expert in the use of their two languages than are these Larkfield children speaking one tongue with their teachers and another with their parents at home. And that is not the worst. Wait until the children are a little older and you shall see them beginning to correct their parents as they are corrected by their teachers, until the rich dialect that should be their proud heritage becomes, instead, a cause for contention and even for shame.

It is so in dozens of cottages to-day. Proud of their new caps and coloured blazers, the scholarship children ride off to the County School, returning home one fine evening well on the way to becoming strangers in the house where they were born.

Well, I suppose it is all one with mechanization and all the other aids of standardization which are the prop and stay of our time, and we but waste our breath decrying it. Nevertheless, thank God, I say, for the untutored speech of such men as Ben and Mark, Sam and Jim Adams, with its firm hold on the things of everyday life, its sensuousness, born of the common clay in which all their days are rooted, and its transparent simplicity.

One of the best places in which to hear such speech is in Sam's forge. Flack the horseman brings one of his mares over from Sandy Ley to be shod; and while Sam is blowing up his fire, sprinkling the fine coal with little shovelfuls of water and raking the glowing heap to and fro, first one and then another look in to pass the time of day. It is warm in the forge and the pubs are not yet open; and anyway, Sam is always good company. Never mind if the place will be smoked out presently, when the red-hot shoe touches the horn of the hoof. Never mind if you will not be able to see a foot in front of you nor if the acrid stench will tickle your throat and lodge a long fortnight in the warp and weft of your clothes. Here is fellowship and talk, and what more can you wish for?

Sometimes Sam is included in the talk; and sometimes, as is befitting to one who bends over the mare's upturned hoof and gives only his broad backside to the company, he is excluded. But the main thing is, Sam or no Sam, the talk goes on.

A moment ago, for instance, Shadwell, the Sandy Ley foreman came in, perhaps to see how the shoeing was progressing, perhaps because he too loves a yarn. Anyway, there he is, leaning against the hatchway. Presently he is seen exhibiting the old broken-tipped spud which he never goes without and which is no small part of the reason why his fields are emptier of thistles than any others in the parish.

"Broke clean in two," I hear him say, between Sam's shouts of "Whoa there, you old b——r," and "Come up, do!": "and you'd never guess how it happened. That spud was given me by Willie Ganer, who was foreman up at Sandy Ley before me. He said he'd had it over forty years; and I've had it these twenty-five. That's sixty-five years old at least she is; and then the other day she went and broke in two, all along of an old bit of sugar-beet. A rum 'un, that was. I was walking through Long Acres, where they'd been taking up the beet, and I went to knock a lump of dirt off one, same as I've done thousands of times.

"Well, dirt weighs heavy, as anybody knows, but who'd expect it to break an iron spud in two? That's what happened, anyway. Just with knocking a lump of dirt off a sugar-beet my old spud broke clean in two. I walked away, thinking about Willie, and how long he'd had this 'ere spud, and how long I'd had it, and what a terrible many days it was since we'd heard a word of the old man.

"And as I went past the house, Miss Mary came running out with a letter flutterin' in her hand. 'Hi!' she called out to me: 'I want a word with you, Shadwell. I've just had a letter to say poor old Willie's dead.' There, wasn't that a queer coincidence?"

The surprise of coincidence may be an easy way of introducing drama into conversation, but it is nevertheless often effective; and certainly few devices of narrative are more favoured by the countryman in a tale-telling mood. One almost felt that there had indeed been some mysterious significance in the snapping of Shadwell's spud, some occult hint of its previous owner's passing. The broken tool, held up for us to inspect, was in some way a degree nearer to animism by reason of the odd coincidence in which it had shared.

Coincidence, then, and next to coincidence, suspense. The most ordinary incident, as an old countryman tells it, will gather interest by dint of nothing else than delay in the telling.

"I was peelin' me taters a-Sunday," said Ann Bright one morning, "same as I be now, and Ted, he was a-sittin' over there in his chair, when I see a motor-car goo past the window, sort of slow, and pull up with a bang. 'Denbys hev got a caller,' I says to Ted. Then Mrs. Banks went hurryin' by—you know how she do goo scanterin' along like a fussy ol' hen; and there was a scrapin' and grindin', and 'No,' I says, 'it's somebody lost their way.' I went to the winder and there was the car backin' right up to our door. I could see a soldier-chap sittin' inside, and 'What in goodness' name do *he* want?' says Ted. 'Why, if that ain't Wally,' I says. And who do you think it was? My gal Annie's boy as I ain't sen for nigh on eighteen years—not since he was no taller'n that ol' lavender-bush beside the door there. 'Granny, how are ye?' he shouts and puts his arms round me. And I cried, and he cried—but there, of course we was only cryin' for joy like. Fancy, now, after all them years!"

A tale of nothing; and yet, as Ann told it, leading up to her climax by repetition of fact after trivial fact, till the sheer intensity of her memory brought the tears again to her eyes, who could fail to share something of her very real pleasure?

But I think what delights me most about country conversation is not so much its dramatic devices, however effective they may be (as some might say) in making bricks without mortar, as in its general flavour.

Inch by inch, these men know the land on which they have worked. It is the main concern of their lives, and nothing about it is too trivial for their attention and consideration. The land— and the men who have worked with them to plough and till and reap it: this is the quiet drama with which they are as familiar as any scientist examining the tissues of life under his microscope.

The land! It decides the slow measure of their tread and it guides their hands, patient and unfumbling, in whatever task they undertake. It monopolizes their thoughts and it colours the words and phrases with which they express those thoughts. It gives their daily bread and takes in return their very lives. Such an absorption is hard for the townsman to understand whose days are spent in a more shifting and varied round of interests. But Jim Adams's "I wouldn't work in a town for all the money in kingdom-come: there's no *life* in the things you have to work with there," sums up almost all there is to say about the reason for this absorption; and no true countryman, with the living earth under his feet and the living fruit of it in his hands, but would wholeheartedly agree.

Larkfield has many an old man and woman whose talk is full of this happy flavour; but for me, from one cause or another, it is perhaps most consistently associated with the countless conversations I have enjoyed with Ben—some of them no more than a word or two thrown over the hedge in passing and others lasting through long lamplit evenings.

Unlike Mark, whose aptitude for drama would secure him an audience anywhere and anywhen, Ben has next to no dramatic sense. He does not seek, by the devices of coincidence or suspension or whatever else, to turn everything he has to say into a story. Indeed, when I first knew him, I thought him unusually shy and even unsociable. Then one evening, after we had been wandering more or less in silence round his garden, examining his crops of pears and plums and apples, he said: "Won't you come inside?" And as we sat round the fire (for Ben, in common with most old countrymen, loves to see at least a spark of fire in the grate even at midsummer) he began a narrative of his life that is now continually having fresh chapters added to it every time I see him.

If I had been wiser, I would have made notes, afterwards, of all those conversations; for Ben's life-story is essentially the life-story of many typical old farm-hands and countrymen hereabouts, and the gathered grain of his talk, threshed of its chaff and cavings, would have constituted a rich harvest. As it is, I must content myself with such scraps as I can remember at a throw, odds and ends which for some reason—a picture, maybe, or a phrase, or a piece of intrinsically interesting information—have defied the curse of an abominable memory.

The only instance I can recall of Ben's ever telling me a story for the story's sake refers to Nick Tyler, an old farm-hand who once occupied the larger of two cottages which, together, now comprise my home. Nick, who is a widower, lived here with his only son Josh, and, on those rare occasions when the sun has power enough to penetrate his rheumaticky bones, he still comes this way and leans over the gate, viewing in a stony silence from which I have never been able to rouse him, the transmogrified home of his earlier years.

"Nick never did much reg'lar wukk," said Ben: "he was what you might call a casual labourer, doing a bit of threshing here and a bit of scything there, everything by turns and nothing long. His son Josh was in the way of becoming much the same. Goodness knows how they did fare sometimes, and it was said, after Nick's old woman died, the cottage got into a rare dutty state. You wouldn't a-knowed it for the same place."

Ben was making his first tour of inspection of my house. He sat on the edge of his chair, a glass of beer in one hand and the worn, shiny handle of his thorn-stick in the other. His keen old eyes missed nothing, and just now he was concentrating their gaze on the big open fireplace to see what device I was employing to keep out the smoke.

"Nick used to do all his cooking—what there was of it!— at that old fireplace," said Ben. "And I recollect they had a little low form in front of it: I think they'd knocked it up for themselves.

"Well, as I was sayin', Nick an' Josh never 'xactly wore their-selves out with wukking; and, whether it were true or not, they had the reputation for putting their fingers on what wasn't their own. Leastways, once when they was doin' a job down at Moat Farm, sawing up some winter wood, the farmer said he'd 'ad about enough of their tricks and swore he'd soon put a stopper to 'em. So he hid in the barn a night or two an' watched where they stole the wood from.

"Then one day he bored a few holes in some likely bits, poured a little gunpowder in, and waited to see what would happen. Sure enough, they took the wood home. On the way they called at the butcher's shop for a bullock's head; and when they'd got indoors, they put it in a pot, laid the fire, and sat down on that old form of their'n to warm themselves. 'Course the gunpowder went off and blew the ol' bullock's head up the chimbley, and Nick and Josh fell back'ards on the floor. Nick was so scared he'd a-given you all the sovereigns 'twas said he'd got buried somewhere out in the fields!

"But the comical thing was that next morning, when he went down to Moat Farm to wukk, same as usual, he told 'em all what had happened and where he'd got the wood from! 'I wonder what could a-been the matter with that old wood?' he said to the chaps there."

Ben's father was one of the last of a grand old line of tenant-farmers, strict disciplinarians both in the house and in the field, mighty drinkers, and devotees of good husbandry. He farmed under the present Squire's father, and it was Ben himself who told me the three conditions which all applicants had to satisfy when one of the Hall farms fell vacant.

"First of all," said Ben, "you had to be a true blue Conservative. Don't, the old Squire wouldn't so much as look at you. Then you had to come of a reliable, churchgoing family. And last: if, you didn't hunt yourself, at least you had to swear you'd preserve all the foxes on the farm. And I wouldn't wonder," Ben slyly added, "if the last condition weren't reckoned the most important!"

"Maybe," Ben said on another occasion, "the old Squire *was* a bit of a tartar. He'd be down on you in a minute if he thought you was letting the farm run away. But I think that was a good system; and, anyway, a farmer fared better under the Squire than he does under the banks that are mostly his landlords these days. Rents were paid once a year, and a rare to-do that was, too! All the tenants 'ld troop up to the Hall and sit down to a feed that lasted half the night: there was pretty nigh anything on the table you could want. But it's all fallen out of fashion now. First it came down to a glass of port and a health to the Squire: now it's nothing at all—the tenants send in their rents by cheque."

Strict as Ben's father was with his children, working them like animals as soon as ever they could use a spade or a hoe, and paying them less than the lowest farm-hand, Ben nevertheless has happy memories of his childhood and early youth.

"I dunno what Tofts Farm looks like these days," he once said to me; "I ain't been that way for many's the year. But when we had it, there was a Glory de John rose rambling all over the front door and a great big ol' Marshy Neal round at the back. Full to everlasting o' roses, they used to be. I'd like to see 'em agen one day, but I don't suppose I ever shall.

"Then there was allus a tame jackdaw flappin' about the place somewheres: I don't remember the time when one or another of us boys hadn't got a tame jackdaw. When anybody called at the house, and stayed for a cup of tea, they used to sit on their heads and start peckin' away pretendin' they was lousy. And once I had a jackdaw that followed me everywhere I went. If I walked down the road, there she'd be, flying about over my head and following from tree to tree."

To children who anyway never went far beyond the parish bounds any stranger who happened to come along was a wonder; and most looked for of all were the visits, year after year, of such familiar characters as tinkers and organ-grinders and fairmen. It was one day when "London George" (as he is called) appeared in the village, pushing his antiquated organ down the street and calling out greetings to his friends, that Ben told me of a man who used to tramp through these villages when he was a lad.

"He was a big man," Ben said: "bigger an' taller than you, and he allus had a bear with him. He carried a long pole and used to make the old bear dance for us, tippety-tippeting about on its hind legs. He waved the stick and sang a little old bit of a song:

Broken windmill under the stars

Don-di-don, don-di-day,
How many eggs can a Jennifer lay?
Six in an hour, ten in a day,
Don-di-don, don-di-day!

"Nights, he used to lay rough anywheres he could get, and I recollect once he lay along o' his old bear in the straw of one of father's barns. I know I couldn't sleep that night for thinking of him out there in the barn.

"Oh, yes, we used to have a rummy lot of chaps call at the farm, one way and another. One night we were told a tramp had gone into one of our sheds. Father went out to look for him but he couldn't see him anywheres. 'If you don't say where you are,' he hollered through the doorway into the dark, 'time I count three I'll shoot.' 'Then shoot, you b——r!' the tramp answered. And then there was a deaf-mute who used to come round begging. He carried a slate with him—so's you could write your answers down. But one day when he came up to the back door, father suddenly shouted at him: 'Stick your tongue out, you!' And the old tramp was so scared he stuck it out there and then. My, and didn't father call him some names after that!"

Farmer Tripp's pride in his horses was a thing that has no counterpart in the farms of to-day. He went everywhere on horseback: he almost did everything on horseback. "He even used to broadcast seed sittin' up on the old mare's back," Ben said. "Eight acres a day was the least he'd do; and the mare would follow down the furrows as reg'lar as if she knew exactly what was expected of her. Father used to hand the mare over to me when he'd finished, so's I could bed her down for the night; and goodness, wasn't she in a pickle—her mane was all full of seeds!

"Father thought he knew all there was to know about a horse," Ben told me one day; "but I remember once when he got let down, nice and proper. He bought a stallion in the market and mighty proud he was when he brought it home. But very soon it began to ail: nobody knew why. 'Here, get up in that manger, boy,' father said to me, 'and pour some of this stuff down his gullet. Let's see if that'll put him to rights.' He handed me the medicine horn and I clambered up into the manger. I reckon I must have fumbled about a bit, for father got impatient and shouted at me: 'Get hold of his tongue, do!' But, dang me, I couldn't find no tongue. 'Come on down, you fool,' father said: 'don't run on so silly, don't.' But he couldn't find no tongue, neither. And what's more, there weren't no tongue to find! It was tore out—and father never knew.

"You see, it had been used as a stud horse before he bought it, and I suppose somebody had tied a bit of cord round its tongue, like they do, to hold it steady when it starts frisking about; and he must have left it there till the tongue withered. You can do anything with a horse if you tie a bit of cord round its tongue and give a tug. 'Course it wouldn't be allowed if the police was to get to hear of it.

"Well, father told me not to let on about it. 'We'll feed him up on some mash,' he said, 'and sell him as quick as we can.' And so he did."

A countryman's knowledge of the locality where he has lived and worked most, if not all, of his days, is so obvious to him that he tends to take it for granted that you must have the same knowledge. You ask somebody the way. "Keep right on as far as Dilly's Farm, then turn in by the old pollard oak there, and make your way over by Gilbert's Meadow"—and all this quite regardless of the fact that you are a total stranger in the place. Similarly, it is seldom the best way of obtaining information concerning the locality to fire off a series of direct questions. The only way of getting to know whatever you want to know is to wait until it comes out by chance in some narrative that probably has nothing to do with the matter you are immediately interested in. I have learned much, one way and another, from Ben; but it has seldom been the result of any direct questions I may have put to him.

"You say you've been all the way to Firkins?" I remember him saying one day; "and how did you get there?" I explained, until I was suddenly interrupted with, "Oh, yes, I know: you went by the dool and through Jesse's Farm."

Dool? I did not understand.

"That's what we allus called it, anyway," was all I could get from Ben, who immediately became confused and evasive directly I queried him about a word he had taken for granted all his life. At last I discovered what he was referring to: a grass path running sheer across an open ploughed field. And with that discovery I had lighted on a link with the days of open field cultivation, when "common balks" gave access to the separated strips, or "selions," which were the peasants' unassailable share in the land.

It was Ben, too, who convinced me that Pig and Whistle, the name by which an off-licence on the outskirts of the parish is known, is not its true name at all. Peggin Whistle he insisted on calling it, and I had to wait months before I learned that this was no mispronunciation. "Peg-in-Whistle" it was, because in former days beer was served in a sort of outhouse there and you had to call for service by means of a whistle which was always kept pegged into a hole in the wall.

A spirit of independence, inherited, it would seem, from his father, is still the most predominant of Ben's characteristics. It asserted itself early in life. At twenty-two, tired of the overwork and under-pay that was one of the major irritations he suffered under his father's strict régime, he ran away from home. It required courage and not a little craftiness, but he found the way. At that time he had a mare of his own and, somehow or other, he persuaded his father to buy her from him.

"Father gave me a cheque," is how Ben tells the tale, "and I went straight off to Melbury to cash it. But the day was Saturday, after the banks were shut; so I went to a lodging, showed the landlady my cheque, and said I'd pay her directly they opened a-Monday morning. As soon as I'd done that, I went up to the railway station and booked my fare to London. Sitting in my carriage, opposite to me, was a young gal name of Sally Pelham. I was so proud of myself, with all that money on me—they shovelled golden sovereigns out to you in the banks them days—that I was soon showing it to her. 'That's a lot of money,' she said, and we soon palled up. When we got out of the train at Liverpool Street, she asked me to come along home with her. But—well, I hadn't been in London afore, and I suppose I was a bit scared; so I never went. But she gave me her address and I remember it to this day: Number 9, Hammersmith Broadway. But I never went there."

His first job was in a carters' yard where he was put on carrying manure. It was easy enough to pick up work in those days. You strolled into a pub, got into conversation with a likely looking man, told him what you were after, and hey presto! there was the job. And of course nobody was more welcome in London in those days of horse-trams and carriers and carters than a well-set-up young man from the country.

What happened to Ben happened to others in this same parish, except that usually it was lack of employment on the land, during the slump of the last decade of the nineteenth century, that drove most of them into the towns. And other old men besides Ben have told me how their prowess with horses served them in such good stead in their new jobs that they often succeeded where others failed.

"I had an old hoss named Tiger," said Ben. "He weren't much to look at when I took him over. I expect that's why they gave him to me! But I soon got him shipshape, and on May Day and suchlike I used to braid and plait and comb him till he looked so fine the foreman said he was the best hoss in the yard."

Five years Ben stayed in London, his jobs ranging from sweeping up manure in the streets to fishmongering. He chummed up with another young countryman and between them they bought an old donkey and barrow in which to hawk their fish round the streets.

But long before the five years were passed, he wished he were back at Tofts Farm. He had neither written nor received any news from home. Fear of what his father would say, and do, if he returned, kept him in London until one day, in the heat of summer, the desire became so strong that he could not resist it. Whatever awaited him when he got home, he must smell again the clean country air and feel the good clay under his feet.

He fell out with his partner. Soon a few pence were all he had in the world. So there was nothing else to do but to tramp the sixty miles between London Bridge and the Glory de John roses at home.

"One would give me threepence here, and another fourpence there," he said. "I lay rough all the way. Mostly I slept out in the barley-fields. Time I got within sight of home, my boots were wore out and I hadn't got any collar round me neck. But oh, wasn't I glad when I caught sight of the old barn and the chimney-pots away across the fields! I saw my brothers carting clover and I went across to 'em and rode home on top of the load.

"I walked into the kitchen and there was father having his tea. He just looked at me over his cup and said, 'So you've come home agen, have you? Get some food inside you, do; and then go and give Tom a hand with that clover.' That was all he said!"

Ben stayed at home after that, married, and lived in one of the cottages on the farm.

If the sons worked hard, so did the father. "The old man never spared himself," said Ben, "I will say that for him!" His only wholehearted relaxation was cards, at which he had sometimes been known to win as much as twenty to thirty pounds.

"There was one farmer," Ben told me, "who lost a terrible lot of money to father, one time and another. He had been a rich man, and I dunno what happened, but I do remember he turned up at the farm one day without a pennypiece to his name. Well, you can tell from this how low down he'd come. Perhaps father felt a bit ashamed when he saw him: anyway, he went and shut hisself up in the stable out of the way. 'Go on, Ben,' he said; 'draw him a glass of beer. I can't bear to see him.' So I did, and when I took it out in the yard to him, 'Hold hard,' I said, 'there's some flies in it.' But he said that didn't matter. He just drank it straight down, flies and all: so you can tell how poor he was."

A game of nap and a bottle of port wine or whisky: these may have been the only pleasures the old farmer allowed himself, but he certainly made the most of them. He went through life with the strength and vitality of one of his own horses; and even the stroke that robbed him of the use of his legs seemed not to diminish him. His last three years were spent in bed, where, propped up against the pillows, he conducted the entire work of the farm with as close a knowledge and as keen an attention as if he were in the enjoyment of youth's own good health. Till the day of his death nobody dared do anything without first consulting him: somehow or other he would discover what was going on.

"He used to carry on cruel," said Ben, "stormin' and ragin' a good 'un. I've known when it's taken four of us, strong men all, to hold him down in his bed. And the night afore he died he asked for a bottle of port to be taken up to him and he drank best part of it himself—nothing would stop him!"

Chapter Fourteen

WE woke yesterday morning to find that the wind had veered round to the west overnight. It became the general topic of conversation: like prisoners released we all took new heart. Sam stopped short in the roadway and sniffed the benign air. "Don't it smell good, midear?" Not that there was any warmth in the wind as yet, for it blew across the whole width of an England buried deep in snow; but at least we could front it with pleasure as we walked down the road.

One of the first signs of this welcome change of temperature was the sudden appearance of icicles, hanging here and there from the thatch. Yesterday they were few and small, but by this morning they had multiplied and become the scenic feature of the village.

If cold weather brings anything more fantastically beautiful than the sight of frost ferns on your window when you wake in the morning, it is surely icicles dangling from the eaves of the thatch, rainbow-tinted in the sun.

Charlie Beslyn, as befits one whose sunflowers in summer are the biggest and whose hollyhocks are the tallest, claims to have the longest icicle of anybody: it hangs from a tiled gully in his thatch, a crystal pointer more than a couple of feet long. But if Charlie's icicles are the longest, then Widow Fields are the most unusual; for, where everybody else's are as erratic in size as in interval, hers hang along the eaves, exactly three inches apart, as if their precision had been achieved with the aid of a foot-rule. The reason is simple: Widow Fields' roof is made of corrugated iron.

Neither Widow Fields' icicles nor Charlie Beslyn's, however, are the ones the children favour. Their attention is solely directed to such as hang within reach of a running jump. The aim is to break off as long a piece as you can. This you proceed to suck, with simulated relish, until your fingers grow so cold that the icicle drops from their hold and breaks into splinters on the ground.

"Now we can look out for trouble," says Mark, voicing the general apprehension that lies behind everybody's smile. Thaw means floods; but before the floods and more dangerous to the traffic is the ice on the roads as the melting snow freezes with the treacherous alternations of temperature. If it was difficult for the tradesmen to get about before, it is even more difficult now, except perhaps in the middle of the day. Beneath the water, inches deep already on road and pathway, there is solid ice that will take days to thaw out of the earth.

Slowly the level beauty of the snow gives place to slush and filth: the ugliness of disintegration replaces the white perfection we have lived in for so long.

A fog lies over the fields, still white with snow, so that one gets the sensation of being at sea. There are no trees, only the sound of continual dripping water, as the icy twigs and branches, hidden from sight, thaw and pit with their quick drops the snow beneath. Birds (they can at least find water to drink now, if not worms to eat) hop about with wet bedraggled feathers, visible for a moment and then lost again in the enveloping fog. In places it is already possible to get a hint of the ruin that has overtaken hedges and stripling trees so long weighed down with the snow. And although that snow still looks solid enough, in track and ride, you have only to put your foot on it and you will sink, suddenly, scrunchingly, up to the knees.

But perhaps the worst thing about this uncomfortable aftermath is the extra strain it puts on people just when their powers of endurance, braced so long, are beginning to flag. It is much more noticeable to-day than it was yesterday, when the mere fact that the thaw had at last arrived was about all that anybody was aware of. To-day the thaw is already accepted and there is a realization that limbs and bodies are being asked to put forward more effort than they can well afford.

All through the thick of the snow Mrs. Swift, who serves her baker husband with a zeal and fidelity no paid hireling would ever dream of giving, has gone about her almost impossible tasks with a smile. Old socks covered her rubber boots, a couple of woollen scarves were tied round her head, and blue fingers stuck out of her mittens, and thus attired she delivered the bread in the village and in such of the cottages outside the village as she could reach on foot. She was forced to discard her trundling barrow, making innumerable trips back to the bakehouse, till goodness knows how many miles she laboured over the snow in the course of the day. Her jokes may have been a trifle heavy, but the merit of such pleasantries is not in their cleverness; and that she still had the heart to joke at all was for me one of the minor miracles of that unkindly season.

One little reward, however, always closed her heavy week.

"Ah, well," she would say, "to-morrow's Sunday, and then I can have a nice lay in. Father always brings me my breakfast in bed on Sunday, then turns on the wireless, so's I can listen to the morning service."

But to-day even Mrs. Swift wears a burdened look as if she had at last come to the end of her tether.

The Swifts' bakehouse stands under the shadow of Goose End windmill. It was a bakehouse when the mill still ground corn from the local fields; and Matthew Pierce, the miller, standing in his doorway overlooking the thatches, must often have shouted a greeting to the perspiring baker in his yard down below. To-day Matthew Pierce lies under the wall of the village chapel, but the baker still comes out into his yard to take a breather after he has put his morning's batch in the oven.

Standing in the bakehouse doorway, Mr. Swift lifts one corner of his white apron and mops the glistening beads from his forehead. His face is round and flabby, not unlike a lump of his own dough which someone has taken and pummelled into the likeness of a spoiled child. He smiles, while the sweat trickles off his eyebrows, but it is a smile that somehow looks more like crying—a misfortune that is emphasized now by the tears of sweat running down his cheeks. Once more he smudges his face with a corner of his apron and then calls out, "Mother! Is my breakfast ready?"

Indeed, to Mrs. Swift the baker is very much the child he looks. This has been her attitude for years, and it is even more so now that the Army has taken away her only son Jimmy.

When Jimmy received his calling-up papers, his father seemed at once to lose all grip on things. "Why should they want to take our Jimmy away?" he asked. "He's all we've got, and what *are* we going to do without him? Folk must have their bread, mustn't they? And I should have thought he was serving his country just as well by helping me and Mother with the bread as he will be kicking his heels in some camp or other."

The fact that Jimmy himself did not seem to mind at all, and that on his first leave home, fatter by many pounds and twice the man he was when he went away, he openly declared himself all in favour of a soldier's life, made no difference: Mr. Swift went on complaining about the unfair way in which these things are managed and the hard struggle it was, now, to keep the business going.

So far at least as the second part of his complaint goes, everybody agrees—and the more so since the snow came. A good deal has been said by our statesmen, since the war began, about the demands which will inevitably have to be made upon the civilian population; and, after the manner of statesmen in moments of stress, they have called upon the classics to bolster up their own inadequacy. Milton's "They also serve who only stand and wait" is an instance. Well, Mrs. Swift has not done much standing and waiting since Jimmy stepped into his uniform, but she has certainly done her share of serving. Even before the war, she was doing her share. If there was a cleaner bakehouse in the locality I cannot imagine it. Every week she scrubbed the troughs and peels and floor, and swept the ceiling, till the place was more like a dairy than a bakehouse.

But now such niceties must sometimes be neglected with the result that, to her annoyance, a cobweb is occasionally seen hanging from the whitewashed beams in the roof, and she may be heard complaining that ever things should have to come to such a pass.

To the scoured and tidy mind of Mrs. Swift a cobweb in her husband's bakehouse is a flag of war.

"There!" she exclaims, doing her best to hitch it off the beam on the end of a peel: "six months ago I'd have called you a liar if you'd said you ever saw a cobweb in our bakehouse. But what am I to do? I'm sure I'm on my poor feet all the hours there are, and even then I'm never finished."

The really distinguishing thing about the Swifts' bakehouse, however, is not so much its cleanliness as its brick oven. Mr. Swift belongs to the old school, and would as soon give up baking altogether as install a steam oven. It was almost as much as he could endure when he finally had to abandon stone-ground for roller-ground flour. He is old-fashioned enough to suppose that stone-milled flour, with all its life (and colour) still left in it, is better than roller-milled flour, white as his own apron the day it comes home from the wash; and that bread baked in a wood oven tastes far sweeter (and is better cooked into the bargain) than bread baked in a modern steam oven.

Leaving aside the question whether he is right or wrong, I for one am glad of his tenacity to the old ways. He is one of the few remaining links we have with those stout, individualistic days when almost every cottage in Larkfield had its own bread oven and almost every cottager baked her own fortnightly batch.

There are still such ovens to be seen in the village, with their close-fitting doors and their watch-stone let into the back wall, by whose glow the housewife could tell whether the heat was at the correct degree or not; but it is many years now since most of them shed an odour of newly baked bread. Like the oak and elm troughs ("trows" as we call them) which once held the family flour and on whose inverted lids the dough was thumped and pummelled into loaves, but which now have either been chopped up for firewood or are debased to such usages as chicken-food receptacles, these cottage ovens are a relic of the days when the self-supporting village was something more than a Utopian dream.

In a corn-producing countryside such as this, therefore, it at least assures some semblance of the continuity of tradition that Mr. Swift should cling to his wood oven. And, as with most traditional occupations, an element of poetry is present which one looks for in vain in modern usages.

I find few village "pictures" more fascinating, for instance, than the prospect of Mr. Swift flinging back the heavy iron door of his oven to see if it is ready for raking out. The whole expanse of the floor, as far as one can see through the open door, is covered with glowing, pulsating ash, a great nest of fiery feathers, throbbing and stirring with heat as if some invisible phoenix were being born out of the livid, flocculent ash, where it would spread its bright wings and issue from the oven door.

In just such a fiery furnace, as a boy, I had always pictured the miraculous adventures of Shadrach, Meshach, and Abednego; and something of the old childish wonder still stirs in me every time I see Mr. Swift fling back the door of his blazing oven. But "Another five minutes'll do the trick" is his only comment on this Biblical scene over which he presides every day. Then he slams the door again and goes out into the yard to get a breath of air.

Matthew Pierce, as I have said, is no longer alive to shout his greetings to the baker over the intervening thatch. Mr. Swift must go to the other side of the parish to get his flour these days, to Mr. Nayland's water-mill below Baldock Rise. It is not surprising the

By the mill-pool

two men should be friends: flour is the trade of both of them and, what is more, both are obstinately attached to the old ways.

If Mr. Swift's trade is no more extensive than it is, much of the reason is to be found in his conviction that, so far anyway as breadmaking is concerned, the old ways were best. If the villagers want their bread baked in the modern steam oven, let them get it from Beavers' bakery: they are welcome—and the implication is that their preference is little to their credit. So young Beavers, gay and noisy and modern, roars round the parish in his brightly painted tradesman's car, swift and capacious and fitted in the most up-to-date, accommodating fashion, mopping up the custom that Mr. Swift is too proud to solicit.

And so with Miller Nayland—or somewhat so. For it is true that he has installed roller-mills in his Doomsday water-mill; but for all that, he quite frankly admits he was happier with his mill-stones.

I remember his scorn one day when I was standing talking with him in the top story of his mill where the efficient-looking roller-mills stand in trim line. First he reached his hand down into one hopper and drew up a palmful of coarse, dun-coloured flour.

"Do you see those little yellow specks?" he asked. "They are bits of wheat germ. All the life and all the goodness of the grain is in them; but no, out they have to come! And for why? Because they spoil the colour. Did you ever hear such humbug? Never mind if all the best of the kernel is there: it spoils the colour, so out it has to come!

"And I'll tell you what makes me smile. When the goodness has been taken out of the flour, to keep it white, the manufacturers sell the germ again as a patent food—a sort of medicine to put right the wrong they did when they took it out of the flour originally. Did you ever?"

Then he dipped his hand into another hopper and pulled out a second palmful. This time the yellow specks were absent: the flour was white.

"That's how flour has to be to-day," the miller said; "else folk won't buy it. White as their own guts!"

Mr. Nayland's water-mill stands on the outskirts of the parish, where our humble river bends an arm round a small hillock crested with a windmill which also belongs to Mr. Nayland. The water-mill is still working, but the windmill stands as idle as old Matthew Pierce's in Goose End. Man and boy, these two mills, the windmill and the water-mill, have been the twin focus of this grand old miller's life. It tears his heartstrings to see that windmill stand idle on its green knoll, for this was his first love.

"They took me away from school when I was a nipper of fourteen," he said; "and at fourteen and a half I was running that mill myself. Yes, sir, fourteen and a half! Of course, father kept an eye on me from the water-mill down here; and if we were very busy I had another lad in to help me, but mostly I did everything myself—ran the whole blooming show. And I can tell you this: they were the happiest years of my life."

But then Mr. Nayland was, so to speak, very nearly born in a windmill. When he was a month-old baby, in long clothes, his father carried him up the mill one Sunday so that this should be the first mill he entered. No wonder he was ready, at fourteen and a half, to take charge of the mill on his own. The swish of these sails, responsive to his command, and the thunder and vibration of the whole massive framework of the mill, as he put on more feed and let the wind have its will with her, are a music that will haunt him to his dying day. "They were the happiest years in all my life."

Yet I realize I must not give the impression that Mr. Nayland is a nostalgic old miller with nothing but disgust for things as they are to-day. He has his memories, and they are happy ones; but he has his quiet pleasure in to-day no less. Indeed, the very fact that his windmill stands idle and his water-mill is seldom called upon to work at top pressure is in itself a sort of compensation. He can take things easily. He still has the satisfaction of being a practising miller, but he has time now to lean out of his dusty windows and watch the pigeons swirl over the mill-tail and settle, one by one, in the neat little cote he has set up for them among the willows. He has time to potter in his garden, time to prune the plums and apples in his orchard close that stands clouded with spring blossom by the river. And he has time to talk over old times when his cronies—Mr. Swift, for instance—come over to see him. Certainly there are compensations in such a 'diligent indolence' in old age, and Mr. Nayland is not one to let them slip by. As for his gruff criticism of things as they are to-day, is that in itself not a pleasurable indulgence? To see such folly going on all around him gives him a kind of superiority.

"Did you ever know such humbug?" he said to me one day as we sat on one of his idle mill-stones while his cats' yellow eyes gleamed at us from among the shadows. "They offered a prize at the County Agricultural Show two years ago for the best loaf made of all-English flour. Some of the women from the village came to me and asked me to mill 'em some home-grown wheat. One of them won first prize. But what tickled my fancy was this. English wheat is no good for bread-making, we are told: must have strong wheats, from abroad. Well, a year after the Show—a year to a day it was—I gave my daughter some of that very flour and told her to bake some bread from it. So she did, and better bread I never wish to eat. Did you ever know such a packet of humbug?

"Besides, if English wheats ain't no good for bread-making, how was it our fathers throve so mighty well on it?—working in the fields all day and eating precious little else."

Foreign wheat, when all the fields for miles around are full of corn, white flour, when common sense tells you that all the good- ness was taken out with the colour—these are often the themes of Mr. Nayland's profitable chatter.

With his one eye he looks out on a world that has gone crazy. Since Doomsday, and earlier, a water-mill has always stood by the elbow of this little river; and, what is more, as far back as records go, there has always been a Nayland in charge of it. A thousand years of grand tradition lie behind the life and activities of this one-eyed miller: is it to be wondered at, therefore, if his thoughts are somewhat caustic to-day when he sees that long line of tradition broken?

Besides, when all due allowances are made for conservatism and old age, there is still so much sense in what he says. White flour and foreign wheat, these are themes that touch the very quick of modern civilization; and although Mr. Nayland is no economist to prove the mysteries of such matters as empire, importation, and high finance, and no scientist, to analyse the precise whys and wherefores of modern diatetic needs, he is wise enough to realize that there is something radically wrong with a world where wheat that is grown several thousand miles away is preferred to wheat that is grown at your own back door, and where flour will not sell until all the best part of it has been carefully extracted.

The heart of Mr. Nayland's mill is the second story, which is reached up a precipitous ladder. Peering through the cobwebs that curtain the windows with their natural lace, you look down on the willow-fringed mill-pond and the flurrying pigeons. The floor throbs under your feet as the mill-wheel turns in the darkness below. Through the centre of the mill rises the mighty wooden shaft on which all the ponderous machinery is geared.

"Yes," said Mr. Nayland, when he saw me fingering the silky surface of that shaft, and examining its intricate grain, "you'll have to go a long way, I'm thinking, before you find a better bit of pitch-pine than that. Have I ever told you where it came from? Although there's always been a water-mill here, it has been rebuilt three times, and the last to rebuild it was my great-grandfather. Somehow he heard of a ship that had been wrecked off the coast—about thirty miles from here. He went down to see her, bought the mast, and there it is!"

Well, from ship-mast to mill-post is not so odd a promotion

as perhaps at first sight might seem: ship's captain and miller have this at least in common—wind and water are the servants of both. Indeed, to run a mill in pre-mechanical days must have been very much like running a ship; and now I come to think of it there is quite a lot of the retired old sea-captain about Mr. Nayland as he lounges round his mill or leans over the mill-race with some friend, filling his pipe and telling of other days.

But it is not the great wooden shaft that makes this second story the heart and focus of the mill. It is the mill-stones, two pairs of them, cased in wooden coffins, with their dusty sleeves trailing over them, down which the grain dropped from the floor above, thence into the waiting hopper, and thence, by way of a continually vibrating "shoe," into the stones.

Have you ever examined a mill-stone at close quarters? Nowadays it is a little unusual to come upon one that is still intact: mostly they have been dismantled and converted into doorsteps, bird-fountain bases, and suchlike alien uses. But if by good chance you should come upon one in good preservation, you will notice at once what an extraordinary pattern has been cut all over its face. The stone (usually built up of slabs of French burr) is chiselled with innumerable sets of close parallel lines called "cracks," of which (at least in the case of the wheat-stone) there are some ten or twelve to the inch. Then there are deeper grooves, forming larger divisions, which go by the curious name of "harps." All told, there are many hundred grooves, large and small, in each wheat-stone.

Why they are arranged exactly as they are nobody knows. Their purpose is to keep the grain moving as the stones revolve, one over the other, and finally to distribute the flour at the periphery.

To keep these grooves chiselled clean to a proper depth was one of the most important jobs in the mill, and it was performed by a man called a "dresser" or "tramping miller." He was one of those itinerant craftsmen whose work, unpretentious and, to the general eye, unimportant, took them all over the countryside.

Sitting on the dismantled stone, with his left elbow cushioned on a bag of bran, the dresser cleaned out the cracks with his mill-bill. All day long the tap-tap-tap of his tool on the hard stone sounded through the idle mill, a strange substitute for the usual roar and under-thunder that accompanied the mill in action.

"Father always hated the tramping miller," Mr. Nayland once told me, "because of course it meant there couldn't be any work done till he was gone again. It took him about a day to dress each stone, and that meant working as long as there was light to see by. You'd think maybe it was a tedious job, tap-tapping all day with your face close up against the stones, to make sure the mill-bill always hit the grooves. But I never knew a dresser complain. In fact, if you wanted to take him off his work before he was finished, because it was getting dark and you wanted to shut up the mill, he only cursed you and just carried on till he *was* finished. That's mostly all a man wanted these days, to be allowed to get on with his job. He hadn't everlastingly got his eye on the clock like they have these days."

For good or bad, Mr. Nayland's mill-stones won't want dressing any more. And for all the handsome profits he makes out of his mill these days he might as well shut it up. The tradition is broken.

When the miller is dead the most probable fate of his mill will be that somebody will buy it and convert it into a domestic curiosity.

What an end to a thousand years of milling!

Chapter Fifteen

AFTER living for weeks in a white, muffled world, it is strange to hear again the sound of running water and to see the green of grass and young winter wheat.

"I saw wheat *growing* to-day for the first time since the snow," says Jim Adams, whose country eye is quick to detect the subtle difference between green and growing green.

But it is the sound of running water pouring off the fields and roaring through the dikes and land drains that announces our release most forcibly. It is as if we had been deaf, and suddenly, in a night, the gift of hearing had been miraculously restored. In mountainous regions, the spring thaw merely increases a water-music that never ceases all the year; but here, where the steepest rise is no more than three hundred feet above sea-level, this gush and splash of water has in it a note of genuine novelty. We lie abed listening to it, judging its rise by minute alterations of tone; children make themselves water-mills out of bits of planed wood and stick them in the balk under the flow from the drains; and as a subject for a passing word it quite outdoes the weather. Only in midsummer, when some sudden thunderstorm breaks the weeks of drought, and the rain falls too fast and heavy to penetrate the iron face of the clay, will this sound be heard again—and then only for a few hours. But now it accompanies our sleep at night, and by day induces a slight and quite unnecessary raising of voices as if in unconscious competition.

And see how the thaw is discovering the farmers' husbandry. In Rainbow Field the wringes of young wheat show clear and bright, but in Tolly's they point out of the water like rushes from a pond. The water stands in the furrows in narrow streams that reflect the sky like blue ribbons stretched across the fields. It cannot run away fast enough, though as you watch it spouting out of the drains and foaming through the ditches you might wonder where it all came from.

Dirty patches of snow are all that are left now in the pastures, whilst even those buttress drifts that flanked the roadside have been reduced to obstinate blocks of frozen snow no more than two or three feet high—waiting, as everybody insists, till the next fall.

The west wind is hurrying spring along as fast as it can: you can feel it already in the unaccustomed strength of the sunshine and you can hear it in the song of the birds. The skylarks are up over the fields around Brock's Hole, binding the clouds with silver chains. The blackbirds and the thrushes have been sadly depleted, but those that remain, veterans of a cruel winter, can be heard at dawn and sunset tuning their notes in the tree-tops. The rookeries are full of strange activity, and the peewits that have flown over the barren fields in flickering clouds are now beginning to separate off in preparation for that nuptial dance when they will call to their mates from the windy March skies and flash the white lining of their wings as they tumble and cry over the fields.

And in Cleavers' pastures, Hod's sheep, heavy with their lambs, kneel to nibble the welcome grass. They have regained a little of that fleecy whiteness which could not compete with the snow. In a week, or less, lambing will commence, and Hod is already putting up the trays and praying that this sunshine will continue so that his ewes may lamb in the open.

It is a crucial time for all shepherds, and most of all, perhaps, for Hod. This is his first season at Cleavers'. I fancy he rather feels he is on his mettle, though you might not guess as much from his stolid, unalterable behaviour. Shepherds are a lonely tribe,

A flock of peewits

whether they work on the high, open downs, far from human companionship, or among the scanty leys and pastures of a corn country. They walk apart from the rest of the men who work on the land, the yellow-eyed sheep their only concern.

And Hod is no exception. When the sheep were grazing in the meadow in front of my house, I used to see him arrive in the morning and stalk through the wet grass among his flock. With his hands in his pocket he went from one end of the meadow to the other, running his eye over all the sheep in turn, missing none, and pausing now and again as something unusual struck him. He knows all his sheep as surely as if the difference between one and another was as obvious as between a Norwegian and a Chinese; and they in their turn as surely know him.

Until Hod came to Larkfield he had never stirred from the village where he was born, fifteen miles away. He knows that all eyes are on him, for all "foreigners" are more or less suspect among countrymen until they have proved their worth. This is Hod's first season and much hangs on it. The more so, as sheep are something of a rarity in the parish to-day. Sheep are no longer folded by the hundred on these fields as they used to be. In a corn country they may be essential to good farming; but, under the present scheme of things, the farmer finds they do not pay; and so good husbandry, as far as sheep and roots are concerned, has to go by the board.

Once upon a time, every farmer hereabouts had his substantial flock. It was integral with his scheme of rotation, and a farm without its flock would have seemed like a garden without its potatoes. But now sheep are a thing to stare at, and those farmers who keep them in anything like numbers are talked of for miles around.

Over in the next parish, for instance, there is a flock of black faces that are as proud an asset to the place as its mythical monster is to Loch Ness. Go to the gate of the meadow where they are folded and see what happens when, for the moment, they mistake you at a distance for the shepherd and come charging over the rise towards you. With the setting sun behind them, each moves in an aura of light. So loud is their collective greeting that the bells of the parish church, a single field away, are not to be heard. And as they crest the rise, converging upon the gateway, it is like all the flocks of Israel being rounded up for a trek into the Promised Land.

Ever since January the shepherd of this Biblical flock has been tending his ewes through their lambing. Straw pens are erected round the stockyard, two deep, and there the puny lambs are first licked on to their feet, where they totter a moment, shaking a tail that is almost as fat as their bodies, and fall. Lambing in the open has been out of the question, with every field buried under the snow, and so the shepherd's hut, with his bottle hanging on a nail by the door and his crook lying against the shafts, stands near by the yard, ready for him to snatch an hour's sleep when he can.

That is shepherding on the grand old scale, such as Mark and others remember here in years gone by.

"But they don't hardly know what the smell of a sheep's like these days," says Mark. "Maybe you don't know it, but there's a power o' good in the smell of sheep. Same as if you've been ill now and was to go and stand up by the fold each morning, and hang about there a bit, the smell'd soon make a man of you again."

I don't know whether Hod has seen this fine flock over in the next parish. Perhaps not; for it seems either to have rained or snowed ever since he first arrived, and, anyway, Hod is a stay-at-home. He lives alone in his isolated cottage on the farm, and a journey across the fields to the pub or to Mrs. Wright's cottage for some tobacco is about as far as he goes.

The day Hod came to Larkfield, rain poured without let. A cottage move is a dismal affair at the best of times; but when there is such unremitting rain as fell that dark, November day, the furniture itself seems to cry aloud against the indignity of the whole procedure. To make matters even worse in this case, the cottage

Hod occupies is approached from the roadway by a narrow chase which that day was little better than a river.

"The places some people choose to live in!" said the lorry-driver, as if Hod were to blame for the cottage being erected where it was.

Hod merely grunted. He was too overwhelmed with the adventure of having moved at all to be aware of the townsman-quips that such a move inspired. Besides, the driver had alienated Hod's sympathy at the very outset: glancing over the shepherd's meagre belongings, before they started on the journey, he had said: "Are you sure you ain't forgettin' nothin'? I don't recollect seeing you put the arspidestra inside!"

And now Hod sat in silence. You would have thought, by the look on his face, that he fancied the prospect no more than the lorry-driver did. But it was not the mud or the rain or the inaccessibility of the cottage that was making him so downcast: it was the unfamiliarity of everything, the slow realization that he was a stranger in a strange land.

"Then it really is true," he seemed to be thinking, as he sat up there beside the driver, staring down the muddy lane to where his new home topped the uncut hedges: "it really is true that I've left the old place behind for good and all? And this is where I'm to live in future?"

"Well, now for it!" said the lorry-driver. "If we sit here much longer we'll be wanting a pair of oars to get you there."

And the lorry splashed its way to the cottage and pulled up before the garden gate. Hod clambered down. His new master was waiting for him in the shelter of the porch, penned in a shower of falling raindrops.

Carrying his crook with him—the symbol of his calling and age-old badge of all his tribe—Hod hurried up the path and shook the proffered hand. The shepherd had come to Cleavers.

That next afternoon his master said to me: "Come and make the acquaintance of a new neighbour of yours."

But Hod and I were already acquainted.

"In you come, sir," he said; and this time there was nothing downcast about him. The reason, once I was inside the cottage, was obvious. The place itself might be strange but the contents were familiar: Hod had spent the wet evening arranging his few belongings exactly as they had been in his old home, and, thus befriended and reassured, had lost something of his perplexity of yesterday.

All told, his possessions did not amount to much: a table, a couple of chairs, a bed, a few boxes knocked together to make cupboards, some bits of china, a radio set, a cat, and some brilliant oleographs. The radio set stood on an upturned orange-box in one corner, the focus of the little room, the Shekinah where dwelt the omnipotent Voice.

But it was the pictures on the walls which Hod pointed out to me with pride. The radio set might fill his cottage with symphonic orchestras and dance bands, but art for Hod was still represented in these homely, shining scenes. "Summer," with fields of ripe corn; "Winter," with sheep in the snow.

"But that one over there is my favourite," said Hod, pointing to a black and white print over the mantelpiece which depicted, with a lurid attention to detail, the heroic endeavour of Jack Cornwall, V.C. "That's a picture, that is," he said, and the glow in his eyes told what pleasure he had had in it as he sat alone before his evening fire.

He poured out a bottle of home-made wine and we sat round the fire, happy enough. And yet, when at length I got up to say good night and left him standing there in his lamplit doorway, some hint of the old perplexity seemed to return. He called his cat inside and shut the door. Who shall say what such a man feels, alone, at sixty, and uprooted for the first time from the village where he was born?

As I turned into the chase I could hear his radio loudly trying to set loneliness at bay.

That was six months ago. Now Hod has neither time nor need to seek comfort from that polished cabinet in the corner. He has his sheep. Few as they are, they represent something in the nature of rejuvenation in Larkfield: they are an attempt, on one farm anyway, to persuade husbandry back into the old healthy rotation. They are a banner stuck up in defiance of the chemicalized farm of the future.

Hod watches the weather in hopes of a good lambing. "Here's luck to you, Hod," I say.

Chapter Sixteen

"HI!" Sam shouts after me as I pass his forge. I cross over the slushy road, and there he stands, beckoning me with a smoky finger. "Hi! Jest you come round here, midear."

And he leads the way round to the shed at the back of the forge, silent and heavy with mystery. It is part of the technique of country conversation never to anticipate, never to show impatience with the slow prelude that will ultimately lead you to the point of the story. To travel hopefully is better than to arrive, says R. L. S., and this is certainly true of nine-tenths of the talk with which Sam and his kin beguile the lazy hours.

Sam unlocks the shed door and waits without comment for me to look inside. Piled on the earthen floor are bushels of potatoes, all spoiled with the frost. They exude a rank odour of fermentation. There must be at least half a dozen bushels—the total yield of Sam's well-tilled allotment.

"Ne'er a blessed tater left," he says. "Did you ever see the like? I had 'em all clamped up there in straw and sacks, till you'd a-thought they *must* be safe. And now look at 'em. I dunnow what we shall do"—and with his heavy boot he kicks the rotten tubers aside.

The action is expressive of his despair. Potatoes are the main-stay of his diet. He savours them as another man might savour his apples. He rubs his great thumb over their harsh coats, weighing them in his hand and appraising them like a judge at the local fruit and flower show. And here they are, the whole of his crop, rotten with the frost, fit only to be kicked aside with the foot.

"And we want 'em more'n ever now," Sam concludes, "seein' as everything is gettin' that dear it's like eating gold."

Others beside Sam are counting their losses now that the thaw has come. After one of the most prolific apple-crops within living memory, there is now a record shortage. In fact, only one thing consoles us as we survey the acrid-smelling mush that was once our apple store—the pigs, so hard to feed now that foodstuffs are almost unobtainable, will have plenty to eat at last.

It wouldn't have consoled Sam, but I, too, could have told him a tale of woe. With a rosy crop that weighed its boughs down to the grass, my favourite apple-tree stood in the sun those first weeks of war, like a rainbow in a stormy sky. Whatever else became difficult to procure, apples would certainly not fail till spring came round again. And friends, fingering them in their nest of straw on the shelves, prophesied that if I ate so many I should begin to look like an apple myself before the winter was out.

And then the other morning I went to examine them and when I had uncovered them I found, not apples, but balls of ice, glistening with frozen drops. I picked one out of the straw and my fingers slid over the sweaty ice. I cut one in half, and instead of the blade thrusting crisp and clean through the firm fruit it squashed into a mess of pulp. These were my apples that had made such a gallant show in the sun! For this my tree had crowned itself with flowers and triumphed over May frosts! I told a neighbour he could have the lot for his pigs and the sooner he fetched them away the better.

It is the same story everywhere. Down in the bar of the Wheatsheaf I hear variations on the same theme, including one on the best way of storing one's crop of apples or potatoes. Luke Negus is telling of somebody he knows who wraps each of his apples in specially prepared paper.

"Don't run on so silly, don't," says Mark; "as if a bit of tishoo paper could keep out the frost. There ain't only one safe way and it's nature's way: make a clamp of 'em in the garden, same as taters."

"Then I suppose your apples have come through the frost all right?" Luke retaliates, somewhat tartly.

"They have," replies Mark; "they have."

Luke is mystified. He passes Mark's garden every day on his way to work, but he has never seen any apple-clamp there.

"Then where did you store 'em?" he asks, anxious to prove his antagonist a liar.

"Where did I store 'em, you say?" Mark pauses a moment and then continues: "Well, I ain't got a tarrible lot of apples, as you know; only a couple of ol' trees and them nigh wore out. Still, they did uncommon well last year and I got 'em stored all right."

"But where?" Luke impatiently intervenes.

"In me belly, you fule!" says Mark over the rim of his glass of bitter; and it is perhaps an indication of the good humour we are all enjoying, now the thaw has released us at last, that this heavy humour wins approval all round.

Released—yes, that is the word. For weeks we have been largely shut off from the outside world, a community that resembled, as nearly as possible in England to-day, the early, self-contained village of our forefathers. We were like a ship in a bottle, and now the bottle has been smashed and the ship is free of the waters once again. Things we were learning to do without, because they were unobtainable, have suddenly become necessities again, now that supplies are renewed; and that contentment we were beginning to enjoy, because to stay at home was the only choice, has vanished now that there are buses and cars on the roads to carry us wherever we wish. In fact we are ourselves again.

Ann Bright stands in her open doorway, who all these weeks has viewed her narrow world from behind spotless curtains. She stands there taking the sun, faint and chill as it is, and will not let you pass. After so long an enforced silence she insists on the consolation of a talk. Whether you desire it also is neither here nor there. And the slightest excuse suffices.

"Go on, you," she says to the despondent ginger cat that rubs against her legs. "Go on, you; I ain't got your kittens." Then comes the story of how she compelled Bright to kill them this morning. "I couldn't stand 'em any longer," she says. "As fast as we carried the kittens out into the shed, the old cat carried 'em indoors agen. And you know, I can't bear to touch they little ol' things; no, I can't." And so Bright had been told to kill them. "Don't, I'll get somebody else to do it," she had said; and her husband, shamed before the taunt of cowardice, had complied. Now the cat is fussing and crying round her slippered feet. "Go away, do," Ann says. "I tell you I *ain't* got your kittens."

Nor is Ann alone in offering her simple salutation to the sun. Throughout the village, cottage doors are open, and here and there you may see men and women peering among the ruck and rubbish of their wintered gardens for the first sight of the forerunners of spring, frail green spears that were cased in ice a fortnight ago and now will soon break into flower. Charlie Beslyn is out in his garden as long as the light lasts, breaking the ground to a fine, crumbling tilth, and little children begin to search along the dikes and roadsides for the first celandines and wild white violets.

Away back in December we even dreaded the approach of spring. Better by far the bitterness of the winter weather than the fate that might befall us with the lengthening of the days. To think that man should ever arrive at such a sorry pass, we said, that he dreaded the coming of spring! But just now it almost seems as if we were wrong. The worst, and worse than the worst, may happen yet; but for all that we find ourselves welcoming the spring after all. Stronger than the dread of war, it appears, is man's happiness in the renewal of earth. The newspapers are full of rumours and the enemy is loud with threats; but the rumour of spring, as the snowdrops push through the thaw, is more insistent at this moment than all the newspapers, and the first thrush singing in the elm-tops is louder just now than all the threats of the enemy.

Later, when the first green rosettes garland the hedges, such optimism will no doubt forsake us—though it will not forsake the thrush. In the hedge by the roadside she will ride her little boat into which she can just fit, tail up at the prow and beak up at the stern, and she will watch you with her bright eye as you peer—not too closely, not too intently, but just for the pleasure of watching and because of the fascination of that brief, slender contact with life of another order, on another plane.

But, although the leaves are green on the thorn-bush and the crab-apple throws its shell-pink petals a few feet farther along the hedge, it will be a Maytime of war; and while the thrush sits there on her nest (her mate not far away somewhere, pulling a worm maybe, tug-tug-tug, out of my lawn and then cocking an ear this way and that, listening for another wriggling, succulent morsel to carry home), the War Department lorries will roar and rumble past, within three or four feet of her; the dispatch rider, with his leather case strapped importantly over his shoulder, will shoot by on his motor-cycle and she will not mind, because she only knows that, whatever they are up to, they are not worrying about her. Better by far, she thinks, the roaring lorry full of singing soldiers and the stinking motor-cycle of the dispatch rider, than nasty schoolboys creeping home along the hedges, looking for nests to rifle, eggs to blow, birds to shoot.

·   ·   ·   ·   ·

There are those who say we should all be glad to be living in this hour. The world is being shaped anew and it is a privilege to be alive while such high things are happening. Well may this be so; yet at this moment I think rather of those who have died already since the outbreak of war, shot down like birds or frozen to death in arctic snows, or cast upon the cold waters to die of exposure or plunged alive to the bottom of the sea, and I wonder what lasting good can come of such violence, such wanton refusal of the life so mysteriously given to us.

I look around me in this quiet village of Larkfield and all I see to-day speaks of life and hope—the spearing wheat in the fields, the audacious snowdrop buds in the gardens, the rising sap in the frail wands of the willow and the dog-wood, the mating birds and the busy farmers.

Only one thing seems in accord with the destruction that is silently piling up the other side of the North Sea.

Twice or thrice a day the timber-lorries splash down the road past my house, bearing the shorn trunks of oak and elm. They are felling trees on Arley Hall estate. Not one tree here and another tree there, but scores of them, massive trees that have breasted the winds of a century and more, bestowing health and beauty with their green turbulence of leaves.

Ever since the timber valuer arrived, weeks ago, these trees have borne on their trunks the earmark of destruction: like those crosses chalked on the doors of the houses of the Plague, they have proclaimed the pity of their approaching end. And now the end has come. First, their stout bases were hacked away, leaving a litter of bright chips scattered on the ground. Then the tree-fellers arrived, with rope and pulley and crane, and one day the mighty tree shivered and cracked and fell, with bleeding branch and twig.

Surely it should be decreed by law, in any civilized country, that for every tree which is felled another should be planted in its place? It is not enough that the Government should make belated amends by setting up trim forests of spruce, regardless of their suitability to the locality, and each planted in a dead straight line with all its neighbours. The glory of our trees (apart from their usefulness) is in their multitudinous dissimilarity, though indigenous to the district in which they grow. And every man whom chance, or ability, has made the owner of wooded acres should, if compelled to fell, have as much regard for the ultimate renewal of the beauty he has destroyed as he has for the cash with which such destruction has rewarded him. Felling trees to pay off debts which cannot otherwise be met is only robbing Peter to pay Paul; and no property can be said to be well-managed where the best of the timber has been felled to pay off debts, unless that timber is at least replaced with suitable and equivalent young trees.

One of the heartening things about the slaughter of trees on the Arley Hall estate is the almost general reaction of the villagers. Time and again, as the timber-wagons sway and rumble past, I have heard expressions of genuine regret that such denudation is necessary. These trees, we all feel, belong to every one of us and we are the poorer for their disappearance. Not even the fact that we shall be able to share in the spoil really consoles us. There will be "tops" at one and sixpence a time—enough wood to keep our fires burning through another winter, whatever hardships war may still bring; and even those of us who cannot afford so small an outlay will have chips by the bushel. But the trees will be gone. A loaf of bread is not always better than a poem, even to a starving man.

So the trees go past, bound for the railway station and thence for the timber-yard. Next to go, we hear, will be the spruce woods—"just the right size for pit-props." Once again the war is denuding the countryside, as it did a quarter of a century ago, of the trees that helped to give us health and sustain our spirits. These are war's scars on the body of the countryside—scars it will take years to heal, if ever.

Otherwise, there is still little enough in Larkfield to suggest approaching holocaust. More lads have gone into the Army to learn to endure their firm young flesh stretched upon the rack of war, and a few older men are volunteering while there is still time for them at least to choose in which of the Services they shall offer to die. Black-outs have all but hardened into a habit and, although we no longer carry our gas-masks, they lie ready to hand for the return of the day when we must. Squadrons of bombers have come back into our skies, but instead of rushing to the window to look at them we merely register the boom of their flight in the pauses of our conversation. Is it a lessening of fear or a gradual acceptance of fatalism? Or merely the sheer impossibility, here in the quiet, awakening countryside, of imagining the full horror of what may befall?

"I ain't goin' to wear no gas-masks," says Ann Bright; "no, that I ain't. There's a little ol' cupboard at the top of our stairs, and I shall hide in there till it's all over. And I 'ont come out for nobody."

Meanwhile, these green spears of life, these fattening buds on the trees—all the frail portents of the resurgence of spring—have an added poignancy this year, an added appeal to our sensibilities. Hod is busy with his lambing and the sight of him slouching through the mud, with a lamb under each arm, its long legs dangling awkwardly against his hips, is somehow sharpened in the mind by contrast with the dark thoughts against which it is set. He is leading his sheep into the fold for the night; dams, heavy with their undropped lambs, and day-old lambs that totter over the furrows on legs that have not yet found their native cunning. The baa of the anxious mothers and the answering bleat of the straying young is as much part of the music of spring as the tentative stanzas of that speckled cock-thrush perched against the sky, and both seem more precious now than ever before.

But most precious of all perhaps is the sight of Jim Adams ploughing in Humpback Field. I expect it is only my fancy but birds always seem to be more than usually plentiful in the fields where Jim is ploughing, as if they knew he liked their company and would do them no harm.

At any rate, all day he has been moving slowly across the field surrounded by a veritable cloud of seagulls blown in from the coast as if, all that distance away, the rumour had somehow reached them that Jim was at plough. There must be well over a hundred. They wheel and cry low over the field till Jim has crested the rise, and then they glide down to the newly turned furrows and settle

The setting sun that brings the labourer home

in thick clots of snowy white. Jim turns at the headland, advancing down the field again; and as the plough draws near they rise, some seeming to wait until the horses' hooves must trample them, and circle overhead, closing Jim in a flurry of gleaming wings.

Here and there among the flashing white horde are a crow or two, croaking mourners at a wedding feast.

"Them gulls are so tame," says Jim, "they just stand there as if it was *you* who'd got to get out of the way! But I recollect a chap once, when he was out ploughing somewhere, chucked a spanner or something at one and killed it—a seagull it was. Well, he never had no gulls following him after that. They stayed over the hedge in the next field and waited till he was out of the way."

Leaving Jim under his cloud of white wings I walk home towards the village.

There are moods of the spirit when the bright, particular things of everyday—houses, gates, the way a tree leans, the motion of a man at work in the fields—seem suddenly of more than ordinary beauty. They are like poems before the poet has spoiled them in the endeavour to chain them with the discipline of words.

I pass a villager pushing a tumbledown pram in which a child sits heaped over with kindling. The setting sun shines in the woman's eyes and something of the madonna shows through the weary lines of her peasant face. "Good night," she says; "good night," and the goodwill that prompts her words is part of the basis of that common understanding (would we but give it play) between person and person, village and village, nation and nation.

I pass lonely farm cottages set back from the road, to whose hearths the men will soon be returning across the evening fields. And they are fixed in my mind as the very type of all men's desire for the fulfilment of his "potentiality to love and to be loved." The faggots leaning against the chimney-stack, the grindstone under the apple-tree in the garden, the few chickens in their run, and the plot of garden waiting to be sown—I see it all as a promise of immense possibilities. Even the brick bungalows, and the staring red council cottages, seem suddenly endearing: homes, loved hearths, centres of that creative love which is the root of all our endeavour, however brief and small.

And as I loiter here and there, talking with first one and then another, I forget for the moment the misery that shadows all our lives in this first faint prelude of spring; I am only aware of the simple happiness that comes of innocent communion, man with man.

In all the shires of England, I think, such cottages wait in the fields and by the roadside, gilded with the setting sun that brings the men home from their work. This is England, though ninety per cent of her population dwells in the towns; for here the first condition of life is not gain but service—service of the land that feeds us and gathers us at last into its fecund darkness. Here men work creatively, ploughing, sowing, harvesting. Here, if anywhere, that goodwill may thrive, which, in spite of wars, shall at last bind the ends of the earth in the bonds of true fellowship.

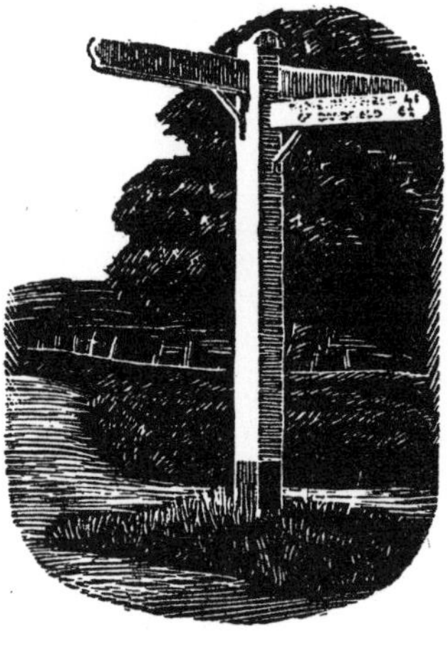